Aspire to Give®

How to Create
a More Meaningful Life
through Your Giving

By Greg Doepke

Chartered Advisor in Philanthropy®

Certified Financial Planner®

To my wife, Suzette;

a Giving Heart that exemplifies selfless giving
to our family, her kindergarten students,
and her many friends.

Thank you, Suzette,
for your example and your enduring love,
support, and encouragement over all these years.

Acknowledgements

The inspiration for this book was derived from my professional experience helping clients financially prepare for, transition into, and navigate "retirement." Although our conversations were focused on their financial lives, I came to know many of my clients and their families on a personal level. I was inspired by their dedication to their families, their neighbors, and their genuine spirit as caring and giving stewards that reached out to those in need. My clients' willingness to serve their families, communities, and their special causes was truly inspirational.

I am deeply grateful to Katie Crew, my editor, who has been with me from the start on this book-writing journey. Katie has been at my side through the trials and tribulations of book-writing and has helped craft the message of Aspire, the Giving Heart and she, too, reflects what it means to give to something greater than self. Thank you, Katie!

Also, thank you, Dayton Cook, Rachael Green, and Joel Moore of Inner Spark Creative for your creativity and professional guidance.

I am also deeply grateful to my co-workers at ACG and the numerous nonprofit and fellow professionals and mentors that give of themselves to their families, to others, and to their communities. The example you set as Giving

Hearts is truly inspirational.

Above all, I am deeply grateful to my wife, Suzette, for her constant love, support, and encouragement. Suzette, is the epitome of the Giving Heart...to me, to her students, to her many dear friends, and to others whose lives she has touched. Suzette is always giving to others and has served as a great giving role model for our family, her students, and her many friends over all these years.

Thank you everyone! I am forever grateful to you for the example you have set for me and so many others through your caring, sharing, and selfless giving!

Let's go do some good!

Greg Doepke

CHAPTER 1

What makes a philanthropist?

There seems to be a very real misunderstanding of what it means to be a philanthropist today. For example, what do you think of when you hear the term "philanthropist?" For most people, through our exposure to daily media and based on what we hear and read, we assume a philanthropist is rich and famous with a lot of money. News outlets readily cover stories of billionaires such as Warren Buffett, Bill and Melinda Gates, and Oprah Winfrey doing their part by donating much of their wealth to the personal passions, causes, and charitable organizations that mean something to them in their individual areas of interest.

According to an article published on www.cnbc.com in February 2018, America's 50 largest charitable donors gave away a whopping $14.7 billion in 2017, more than doubling what was given the year before. While Bill and Melinda Gates top the list with a $4.8 billion donation to their foundation, a noticeable shift could be seen with younger tech giants like Facebook CEO Mark Zuckerberg and Michael Dell rounding out the top three spots on the list.

The idea that to be a philanthropist, one must be in the top tier of wealth as billionaires and millionaires is perpetuated and portrayed regularly through a variety of mediums including movies, articles, books, TV specials, and other media. The news stories of the world's wealthiest giving it away to those who need it to inspire others to do the same can convey a narrow and misleading interpretation of what it means to be a philanthropist.

Let me clearly state that you and I and most everyone are philanthropists in the real world. Taking it back to the basics is a good place to start. If you look up the word philanthropist, the definition clarifies it is the love of humanity and the altruistic giving of your heart to something outside—something beyond—yourself. This can include giving to your family, friends, and neighbors. It can be extended to total strangers in your local community. So, you see, if you care about someone or something else and you give of your heart to improve the state of life for another person or cause—you are a philanthropist.

We all know philanthropists in action within our local community. They are our spouses, neighbors, professionals, teachers, and business owners demonstrating through their generous giving that they care, and hence they give. For example, there are a multitude of retired teachers—like my wife Suzette—that volunteer on a regular basis in local schools by reading to students and helping teachers with other classroom needs. Retired nurses may volunteer at the hospital taking meals to patients and spending time with them. Examples of these philanthropists in action are all around us.

Let me share with you a true story of someone who has been an inspirational example to so many (including me) in a local community. When we first moved to Virginia, we found our dentist who was in the initial stages of what was to be a very successful dental practice. What is especially noteworthy is the example that he set for his dental clients, his employees, and all who knew him. Over the years as his professional dental practice grew, he also became well known locally as an exceptional watercolor artist. As his reputation grew as a dentist and an artist, he combined his professional and personal loves in a way that benefitted his local community—his "hometown." As an active alumnus of a local university, he began to donate his artwork to the local dental school. His alma mater would, in turn, raise funds by auctioning off his much-in-demand artwork. It was a win-win for all! My dentist would passionately brush his canvas using his talents, give the finished artwork to an organization he cared about, and they would benefit from his generosity. And yet another giving heart contributed to a cause they believed in and would purchase a one-of-a-kind piece of art! Everyone would feel good about and benefit from the dentist's giving heart. My dentist would feel the satisfaction of his painting and his generosity, the university would raise funds for the dental school, the buyer of the artwork would feel good about their financial generosity, and future generations of dentists would receive the benefit of the professional training. Talk about a great "let's do some good" story!

The key takeaway from these stories is this: we don't have to be mega-rich to be a philanthropist. We are all philanthropists if we care about something greater than self and if we unleash our inherent need to give in a smart, impactful way, good things can happen. Discovering the best way to use our gifts to reach out, make a difference, give back, and do some good that is outside of self is what smart, meaningful giving is all about.

Now that you are realizing your own potential as a philanthropist, you may be asking yourself, "What can I give?" The answer to that will vary as much as each of us varies individually as giving hearts. But there are also threads of commonality weaving a tight-knit blanket surrounding us all on the philanthropic frontier. In fact, we routinely hear of the ways we can give of our time and give of our talents—our skills and expertise. We can all give of our treasure—especially if we are fortunate enough to have such treasure—like financial resources, real estate assets, and other possessions, which is a broad category encompassing even our gently used belongings for in-kind donations. The fourth and final area of giving—that we as giving hearts, as philanthropists—can offer is trust. What do you mean by "trust" you may ask? In the context of our giving hearts, trust is our relationships with other people that we have developed and strengthened throughout our lifetime. The giving of trust is a concept we will discuss in more detail later as there are many interconnected, moving parts forging trust.

Have you found yourself on the edge asking, "What now?" Well, now is a good time to recognize and unleash your giving on your own life journey. We can't begin to imagine what your life's journey has been, is and what it will be, but we hope—we aspire—to help you find your way on a fulfilling and beautiful path. For the path of giving—of being a giving heart—goes beyond you and your family. At Aspire to Give, we realize that those with awakening giving hearts may need a helping hand as they start to discover what their giving will mean to them, and one way to do that is to use both your leading, giving heart and thinking head.

What about YOUR life journey of aspirational giving? The answer will become clear as we each start uncovering our personal gifts for giving. But first, let's explore that common thread we all have—our life's journey.

CHAPTER 2

Our Common Life Journey of Aspirational Giving

Throughout the 20 years I have helped clients prepare for, transition into, and navigate retirement, there was one overarching need that became obvious and it was not based on any financial issues. That glaring need was the change going from a career, family raising, and having a busy—sometimes hectic—lifestyle to a significantly different version offering the freedom of choice in how to spend one's time and what to spend it on.

In my conversations with clients I often shared with them that to have a successful retirement, three things are needed. These three things are: structure, engagement, and purpose. The structure being your daily schedule; engagement being the social interaction you have with others; and third, what is your purpose in this new phase of life? Why do you get out of bed every morning?

My clients were caring, loving, and generous people with true giving hearts who were very inspiring in the way they served their families, their communities, those in need, and those causes and passions that were meaningful to them. Such is the origin of the life journey of aspirational giving. We all remember the bell curve. I oftentimes referred to it when clients and I would discuss the accumulation and distribution of financial assets for retirement. We spend our time accumulating funds and then distributing them during retirement. This distribution combined with the uncertainty of what retirement holds for many people and their inherent nature to give of themselves prompted me to do some additional reading and research on the motivation of giving.

Hence, I started reading about Abraham Maslow. I remembered learning about Maslow's hierarchy of needs when I was in 6th or 7th grade. I decided to read his book, The Farther Reaches of Human Nature, which was published in 1971 just after Maslow's death. He introduced the concept of self-transcendence. As you may recall, Maslow had this hierarchy of needs going from the basic physiological needs like food and water to safety and security to love and belonging to esteem and accomplishments and finally to the top of the triangle with self-actualization. In this last

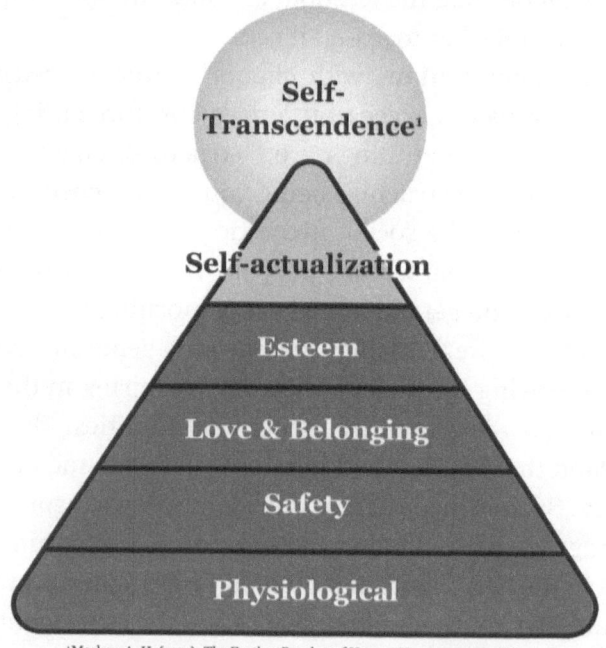

[1]Maslow, A. H. (1971), *The Farther Reaches of Human Nature*, pp 259-286

book of Maslow's, he introduced self-transcendence as a continuation and extension of self-actualization, which is about achieving and reaching your full potential. Maslow's introduction of self-transcendence takes it a step further, and for some people, giving of themselves or transcending becomes the highest of human needs.

In my readings, I was once again reminded of another book I read about 15 to 20 years ago—Viktor Frankl's Man's Search for Meaning, which is about his time spent in the concentration camp during World War II. I decided I wanted to read more of his work, so I ordered and read The Will to Meaning: Foundations and Applications of Logotherapy. In this work, Dr. Frankl refers to logotherapy as finding meaning in people's lives even through the hardest of times. Once again, like Maslow, Frankl clarifies that self-transcendence is reaching beyond your needs. It is the giving of yourself to something greater than self that brings meaning to your life.

This brings me back to those people on the verge of retirement trying to find the meaning in their lives after their career. I also thought about what it means to give. We typically think of giving of ourselves in terms of the giving of our time, talents, and financial resources. One gift that is not mentioned often that is just as important as any other is the giving of trust. These are the trusted relationships we each establish over our lifetime. This brings me back to the curve. If you view the bell curve (shown on the next page) as a representation of our life's journey—the common life journey we all travel—the left-hand side of the bell curve reflects an accumulation (#1).

The Life Journey of Aspirational Giving

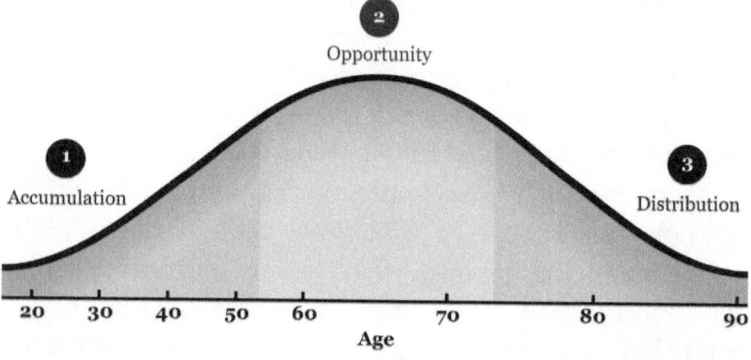

What I mean by accumulation is that in our 20s, 30s, and 40s when we are novices in the scheme of life, we are building our talents through education and gaining new skills and experiencing life as we know it. This part of the accumulation curve also reflects the accumulation (hopefully!) of our treasure—our financial resources—such as rising income and savings, building a business or professional practice, and purchasing a home. It is also during this accumulation phase that we are building trusting relationships, such as marrying the love of our life, raising our children, enjoying a growing family, and building neighborhood, community, and professional relationships. If we are so fortunate, we find mentors and others that show us the ropes and how to navigate, whether that be with family life, raising children, marriage examples, or professional career mentoring. If we can find trusted relationships in all of these, then they become valuable, and they become part of what we call at Aspire to Give, our "giving wheelhouse."

Our giving wheelhouse is a composite of all the gifts that we have in terms of time, talent, treasure and trusted relationships. We spend this time, the first 50 to 55 years of life, which varies from individual to individual, accumulating our relationships, accumulating our treasures, and accumulating skills, life experiences, knowledge, and hopefully some emotional intelligence along the way. You'll note that I did not include time. For it is during this accumulation period that we do not have a lot of time because we are investing our time in our families, in our relationships, in our careers, and living life doing what we do each day at home, at work, and in the community we chose to raise our families, live, and play.

So, by the time we get to mid-life, we have some years, lessons learned, and life experience behind us. We ever so slowly start thinking about life after career, life after kids, and what we will do to fill those hours and still have a purpose and meaningful and fulfilling life. Based on my experience providing retirement guidance for my clients, I read yet another book. Joseph F. Coughlin founded the MIT Aging Lab in Massachusetts and he authored a book called The Longevity Economy in which he addresses the growing lifespan of individuals due to better health, advancing medical technology, and other reasons from which we may have an extended and healthier lifestyle beyond our career.

In his book, Dr. Coughlin mentions that in our current media, there is a tremendous amount of marketing products and services that address the bottom portion of Maslow's hierarchy of needs—the safety, physical security and even the love and belonging portions of our needs. In looking at all these factors, my experience with clients, the transition into retirement, and the uncertainty of a purpose for people in retirement, there is an obvious void in meeting the highest of all human needs—the aspiration we all have to give. These reflect our transcendent needs. Hence, as we transition into retirement, we enter the opportunity phase of life. By the time we reach age 50-55, we have accumulated a multitude of tools. These tools include the talents gained from education, skills, life experiences, and life-lessons learned. Hopefully, we have accumulated financial resources for retirement and, if we are so fortunate, there may be more than we need. We have also established relationships through our working careers from which we can tap as potential resources. Unlike the accumulation phase when time is not available, during the opportunity phase and with increased longevity, we now have the time to spend time with children, grandchildren, friends, and giving to those causes and passions that are important and meaningful to us.

As you can see, the bell curve reflects a third phase of our life journey—the distribution phase. During the distribution phase, we think of passing our gifts to our family, friends, and communities in a way that reflect our value system and we strive to serve through mentoring, guiding, and coaching. It is also a time when we are required to distribute our financial resources either to ourselves, through gifting, as income from our retirement (401k, IRAs) savings or at death. We become more interested in creating both a living and lasting legacy by perpetuating personal and family values and traditions.

There you have it in a nutshell—the life journey of aspirational giving. This life journey is common to all of us. We each have an inherent desire to give of ourselves to others and to causes, or passions that are important to us. For it is our giving that brings us meaning and purpose in our lives. It becomes obvious that there are three phases: the accumulation phase, the opportunity phase, and the distribution phase. During the first half of life when we are accumulating our relationships, our financial resources, and our talents, we are using our time to accomplish these ends. We then approach the end of our career and, for some of us, we realize that our children are grown and have moved out, raising families of their own. Typically, in mid-life, we begin to look in our crystal ball and reflect on the multitude of opportunities that lie before us in our remaining years. We assess our lives and may realize that we will have the freedom to help our children, spend time with grandchildren, to pursue our other dreams, and to give back to better our communities. We realize that there will be newfound freedom and that we now have the opportunity and the time to "do good." We may be fortunate enough to have longer, healthier lives and recognize that these accumulated gifts can bring meaning to our lives, purpose to our day, and ultimately benefit others. This transition from career to calling is a great opportunity for all of us and Aspire to Give's purpose is to bring meaning to people's lives by helping them navigate this transition.

CHAPTER 3

Your Giving Wheelhouse
Your Gifts for Giving

What are our gifts for giving? If we each take a moment to reflect, we may realize we inherently know exactly what it is we have to give. It may have been lingering there just under the surface of our subconscious as we plowed through our daily lives. And now as you find yourself front and center on the tranquil mid-life stage, you hear that inner voice saying, "You have so much to give—your time, talents, treasure and more..." Listen to that voice. Understand that we all have something to give and that our gifts fall into four main categories, which is our giving wheelhouse. This giving wheelhouse—while unique to us individually—consists of the same tools for us all: time, talents, treasure and trust.

Let's take a broad look at each of these four gifts for giving in our giving wheelhouse.

Time

"Volunteers are the only human beings on the face of the earth who reflect this nation's compassion, unselfish caring, patience, and just plain loving one another."

-Erma Bombeck, American humorist and author

How do you use your time? Think about it. Is it time well spent? Is it full of activities, tasks, and events that are for the most part fulfilling? How you use your time is a key reflection of who you are. Like most of our personal gifts, we can squander it, or we can use it for personal satisfaction, spend it with family and dear friends, invest it in ourselves and our future. We can give it in service to others. How we use our time reflects who we are and who we will be. It is important to pause, take stock and make sure we are utilizing our time in ways that better us, our families, our neighbors, our community, and the lives of others.

I would argue that our time is, in fact, the most precious of all our gifts. Why do I say that? Simply because our investment of time is the vehicle by which relationships, ideas, impactful programs, and ultimately results are achieved. Investing our own personal time in building relationships is the foundation by which we make vibrant, successful, and prosperous families and communities. It is also the equalizer among our gifts for giving. You see, we ALL have the same amount of time—day in and day out, year after year. Time as an overall component of our giving plan is the same for us all. We all have 1440 minutes in a day—24 hours—to make the most of. How will you choose to use your time? Assessing how you use our time is only part of the fun you will encounter on your life's journey of aspirational giving.

Talents

Another tool in our giving wheelhouse—one that is not dispensed as equally as time—is our talents. Talents, simply put, are our skills and expertise. Talents may evolve, change or develop at various stages in our lives and in varying degrees. They can also come in various forms. Our talents are born from our natural characteristics, inclinations, and attitudes. For example, some of us are naturally creative and intuitive. Others may have a knack with numbers and organization. These inherent traits are the precursor to potential further development thus giving way to one set of talents. Also included in this category is our education from kindergarten to college to our professional development and continuing education. We also learn through meeting personal and professional challenges in life; as well as through other experiential life lessons learned.

Talents can come in the form of skills we develop through personal experiences, which shape our attitude and how we approach and handle varying situations. Those experiences can be broad and ever-changing. They can be grounded in a professional career, or careers, or rooted in the life experiences of raising a family—just living—and continuing our life's journey. We each have life lessons to grow from and we develop talents in collaboration with the shared experiences of others. Throughout our lifetime we may acquire a wide range of abilities that may or may not be consistent with our natural born aptitudes. When reflecting on your individual talents, it is important to remember this far-reaching spectrum should ultimately be aligned with the passions and causes that mean the most to you. Think about how your gifts can be used to better those things—to contribute in the most impactful way—to those causes that are important and meaningful to you.

Treasure

On the surface treasure—our money—may seem like the easiest to understand. While money is the easiest to conceptualize as treasure is tangible, it is truly one of the more complex gifts in the giving wheelhouse. In a nutshell, treasure deals with the financial resources that we have available to us individually. These financial resources can take on many forms including financial assets, real estate property, the value of our business assets, and other nontraditional financial resources. These can include in-kind donations, gently used property and collectibles. All of these are part of our financial resources, our treasure, or "money."

Money, or treasure, is also very close and personal to each of us. Because of the role money plays in the daily exchange of our lives—both present and future—it may be considered by some as the most valuable of our assets. It is through the exchange of money that we provide for ourselves, our families, address our needs, our wants, wishes, and for some, use it for the good of others.

Our personal financial resources as a gift for giving may take several forms. Most of us tend to think of the typical nonprofit request for money as a charitable donation. The donation may be in the form of a check, an online donation, or an extra dollar or more at a local store for a specific cause. However, personal financial resources may also include other less top-of-mind substitutes such as appreciated property or stock, the value of a business, collectibles of some kind, gently used property, or in-kind donations. Your personal financial resources as a gift for giving may be in various forms. Our treasure, or "money", is quantifiable, real, relatable and ever so top-of-mind awareness as reflected in our daily lives and in the media.

Trust
(our relationships with others)

The last personal gift for giving that we each have is typically the most overlooked, yet still extremely meaningful to each of us, and this is our trusted relationships. We build a variety of relationships with the people that have crossed our paths in life at some point. In the early years, our trusted relationships include our parents, immediate and extended family, teachers, youth coaches and role models, and childhood friends and their parents. As we leave high school and enter adulthood, we develop trusted relationships with college roommates, teachers, coaches, mentors, bosses, and educators that have taught and inspired us. Many times, we take these trusted relationships that we have developed and let them wither and fade away as our life journey moves on. We are so very busy during this accumulation phase! We may not have the time or inclination to seek out, nourish, and maintain trusted relationships. We may not understand the importance and role of trusted relationships as a gift in our wheelhouse. But we do not travel on this road of life alone. It is with the support, encouragement, development, inspiration, and resources of others that enable us to go about our life's journey in raising our families, developing our talents during our careers, and making an impact on those around us. These truly trusted and maintained relationships are overlooked as a personal gift for giving but serve as a resource for other gifts that others may bring to the table.

To clarify trust as a gift in our giving wheelhouse, let me share with you a personal example of how a trusted relationship can serve as a gift. For the last 20 years, I have developed a professional relationship with Teri Lovelace, a true inspirational philanthropic leader with a giving heart that I first met when she worked as the senior philanthropic advisor with the Richmond Community Foundation. Our common excitement for leading-edge philanthropy was mutually reinforcing when we met over coffee about every six months. Teri eventually left the community foundation and went to serve as chief impact officer with Virginia Community Capital and then helped establish and become president of LOCUS Impact Investing, a firm whose mission is to empower place-based foundations to invest their capital locally to build prosperous, vibrant communities. Teri and I continued to meet for coffee about every 6 months to discuss the exciting opportunities of leading-edge philanthropy.

After moving to Auburn, Alabama, I became involved with the Auburn University Women's Philanthropy Board, the flagship division of the Cary Center for the Advancement of Philanthropy and Nonprofit Studies. I volunteered to serve on their board. Kim Walker, director of the Women's Philanthropy Board, was seeking a symposium speaker for their 2019 annual spring symposium. I suggested Teri be invited to speak. Teri accepted the invitation and shared her experience, knowledge, and wisdom regarding the philanthropic leading-edge concept of social impact investing with the well-attended audience.

This story highlights the importance of the resources we can bring to our passion and purpose through the trusted relationships we have with others. Understanding and enlisting our personal and professional network—our trust tree—in meeting resourcing needs is a true gift for giving from our giving wheelhouse. In this story, Kim was looking for an outside speaker to bring a new perspective and speak about leading-edge philanthropy. With Kim's trust in me, and my trust in Teri, and Teri's trust in both of us, we were collectively able to bring additional educational content to an audience that was enthusiastic to learn and become aware of this leading-edge philanthropic tool of place-based social impact investing.

It is vitally important that you recognize, nurture, and enlist the personal, community, and professional connections that you have. With our inherent need to give, we can reach out to these trusted relationships to bring other's gifts of time, talents, treasure and trust. If we open our minds, recognize the resourcing possibilities that we may have in our trusted relationships, and reach out to engage those relationships, each of us can change our corner of the world for the better.

CHAPTER 4

The Need for a Process and Intentional Alignment

As I myself turn the page from a 20-year career of advising clients that are approaching, transitioning into, and navigating retirement, I have become keenly aware of the need for a process. What do we mean by a process? In this particular case, we mean a guided, comprehensive transition as you move from a 30-year focus on family, career and a busy daily routine to the slower pace of an empty nest and free time in retirement. I have become painfully aware of the tremendous unmet need for non-financial retirement guidance and coaching that is not being addressed by professional advisors (nor should it be). It is normally not the professional advisors' job to help you figure out what your non-financial life in retirement will look like. You, and you alone, are the captain of your retirement ship and, for most, a process is needed to navigate the transition from the known past to the uncertain, unknown future.

We are all on a life journey and I have shared with you the phases, the research, and the opportunities that we each have as we transition to the next stage of life. As we make this transition in the opportunity phase, we are each in a position to make a real, authentic difference in the lives of others and the causes that are important to us. Currently for this transition to retirement, the emphasis has been on the financial transition. Additional, more comprehensive help is needed for the non-financial, exciting and, in some ways, scary life milestone we call retirement. While the 6-step financial planning process outlined by the Certified Financial Planner Board of Standards may be suitable for income and financial security, it is solely focused on the financial aspects of this transition and does not address the important and meaningful non-financial aspect of our transcendental higher giving needs. Those giving needs include our desire to care for family, others in need, and our environment.

To meet these non-financial, higher level, transcendental giving needs, a process is needed. We need a methodical approach to define and align our purpose with our passion and thus provide meaning to our lives. This need can be defined as follows:

"As we aspire to give, so shall we aspire to become on our journey to make better..."

To add additional clarity, we each have this intrinsic aspiration to give of self. If we can become better givers of self, then we can make better or improve those conditions or causes that are important to us. By becoming better givers, we can do more good!

Since we have this inherent need to give, our goal in retirement is for each of us to become better givers to family, friends, community, and important causes so that we can do our part in making something in our world better. By using this process and this aspirational goal that is intentional, purposeful, and meaningful, we can have a clear-cut path on our own journey to smart and impactful giving and very fulfilling years of retirement. This brings us to the power of intention.

The Power of Intention

As clearly stated, there is a tremendous need for process if one is serious about their own gifts for giving and making a difference in the lives of others. What do we mean by the power of intention?

This is a unique concept explored in detail in a book by Dr. Wayne W. Dyer, The Power of Intention. The premise is that intent is not something you do, but something we are all a part of. Dyer explores the power of intention as a force of energy that we can access and harness to co-create our lives. Dyer is a man worthy of quoting and one such quote that applies to us in the context of giving and living with our best intentions is below:

> *"The measure of your life will not be in what you accumulate, but in what you give away."*
>
> -Dr. Wayne W. Dwyer (Staying on the Path)

The power of intention is critical for effective, smart, and impactful giving. What is your intention in your giving? What is the desired impact you hope to have from your giving? If we understand the importance of intentional giving, then we can most certainly understand the need for a process.

We must first realize our giving reflects the totality of who we are, the experiences of our life's journey, and the important people in our lives whether that be our parents, siblings, teachers, mentors, coaches, or others. Because we are dealing with the totality of who we are as individuals, the intentionality and the process must consider what I call the "Giving Heart" and "Thinking Head." It is a composite of our emotions (our heart) and our rational decision-making process (our head). Whether we believe it or not, our decisions are led by and motivated by our hearts. Our hearts, and therefore our emotions, are what really drives us to do what we do. For those thinking that they are strictly rational in their decision-making, think again. It is with a light heart that I suggest those rational individuals are channeling all their emotion into convincing themselves they only use their head in decision making—no emotion needed. So, we must start with the premise that all our decisions are led by emotions—our heart—and we then are rationalized with our thinking head.

The Need for Alignment

Thus, we have shared with you the need for process and the need for intentionality. What are we being intentional about? At this stage, let's introduce the concept of alignment. Specifically, it is through an intentional process by which we strive to align our purpose with our passion. I encourage you to take some personal time to reflect on your life at this particular stage. If we each reflect on what is important to us, our individual giving wheelhouse, and the passions that develop from our personal and professional life experiences, we can then apply a process to understand and align our purpose, our passion, and our giving. With the intentional focused alignment of all three components—our passions, our purpose, our gifts—we identify the "sweet spot" from which we can pursue our dream to make the greatest impact in service to something greater than self. This laser focus and alignment provides us with the awareness and motivation to pursue our dreams of making better something that is meaningful and important to us.

As you'll see from the next chapter, we have developed the Appreciative Donor Education Process that, at its core, serves as a tool to assure our giving is intentional, aligned, and personally meaningful.

CHAPTER 5

The 5 Steps of the Appreciative Donor Education Process

From my professional practice, when people think about, approach, and transition into retirement, it seems that—for many people—they are entering a twilight zone. Without a clear direction and purpose, and with the anticipation of total time freedom, they blissfully drift into a lifestyle that is vague, uncertain, exciting, and—yes—even a little scary due to the unknown. After all, they have just been busy in their lives, raising families, building their careers or businesses, and adding to their inventory of skills and talents through education. At some point in our life, typically mid-life, people start thinking about retirement and what they're going to do wondering what "retirement" looks like. For people that are fortunate enough to have more than enough financial resources, finding a new purpose is a big part of the unknown and may be the biggest challenge. As shared with clients during the last 20 years, it pays to reflect on finding answers to the non-financial needs of retirement. During reflection, it helps to break down those needs into three main categories: structure, engagement, and purpose.

- **Structure:** what is your day going to look like?
- **Engage:** how will you engage with other people?
- **Purpose:** why do you get up in the morning?

After seeing so many people approach and face their transition and struggle with a life's purpose after a career, there is an obvious void and real need for people to find their purpose; especially since they may very well have another 10, 15, or even 20 years of productive life. In my multitude of conversations with clients, many of them voiced their inherent need to give. Their giving may include spending time with their grandchildren or seeking to unleash their potential to give back to their community to make a difference. In these philanthropic conversations, I have found that many people—most people in fact—are generous and as they transition into retirement or the next phase of life, they are going to have the time to give back. They have giving hearts and they're looking for purpose and with purpose comes meaning. Clearly, most people facing retirement are facing an unknown and are looking at how they can really enjoy and have a meaningful and impactful retirement.

Having a "process" background in one of my prior careers, I understand the importance of establishing a roadmap for people to make this transition. The roadmap is simply a process for getting from an extremely busy, known life of raising a family and career building during the accumulation phase of life to a vague, unknown life beyond work where one has flexibility, freedom of time, and freedom of choice. What is this process for this transition? In doing some preliminary research, I discovered the power of Appreciative Inquiry (AI). For those not familiar with the Appreciative Inquiry process, it is a process that engages individuals and groups in self-determined change. It revolutionized the field of organizational development and was a precursor to the rise of positive organizational studies and the strength-based movement. It was developed at the Weatherhead School of Management at Case Western

Reserve University in the 1980s by two professors, David Cooperrider, and Suresh Srivastva. It seems that the emphasis on "problem-solving" was hampered by any kind of improvement in the individual as well as a social improvement so they created new models of inquiry that focused on the strengths of the individuals, the strengths of the groups, the strengths of diversity, and the strengths of perspective. It is a life-giving, strengths-based approach that helps people focus on what they do well and how one's talents and energy can be channeled for his or her own good and therefore the greater good of a group, cause, or passion. The key word to focus on in the process is strengths—with the ultimate goal being to improve upon and leverage your existing strengths.

The Appreciative Donor Education Process

In looking at the needs for the transition to retirement, this AI model serves as a great foundational tool from which to build a comprehensive and integrated process to help people make this transition. With our inherent need to give and with the personal search for purpose in retirement along with increased longevity, we extracted the positive, life-giving, aspirational elements from the AI process to develop a new process to help pre-retirees transition to their new phase of life which we typically call retirement. It is a tool that helps them discover their life's purpose and lay out a roadmap that incorporates their desire to give to their families, as well as give back and bring meaning to their lives. This process is reflected in the diagram of what I have termed and coined as the "Appreciative Donor Education Process."

The Appreciative Donor Education Process

This process can be used at any time during one's life but is most applicable at the opportunity phase of our life journey. It is most effective at the end of our careers and in our early retirement years while we still have our health, resources, and new time-freedom to make a difference with our families and in making the world a better place.

Let's take a closer look at the above process model. These five steps include the components of discovery, dream, design, delivery, and destiny. In consideration of our giving heart and our desire to make a difference while creating both a living and lasting legacy, the process starts in the center with a specific definition that is targeted to philanthropic giving.

Definition

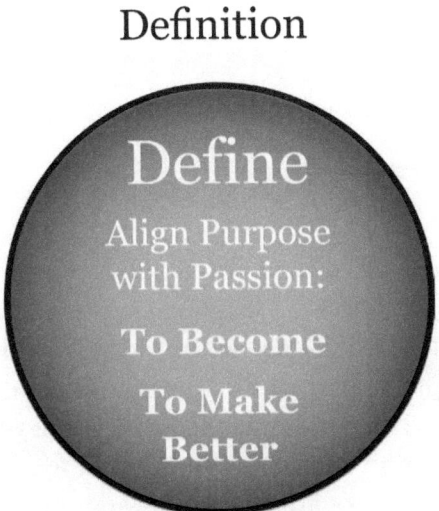

The definition of this Appreciative Donor Education Process can be best summed up with the aspirational, intentionally aligning, and life-giving phrase:

"As we aspire to give, so shall we aspire to become on our journey to make better..."

This defines our purpose during this transition period from which we begin our philanthropic giving journey. We choose the positive as the focus of our inquiry and build upon and leverage our own unique life-giving strengths.

Discovery

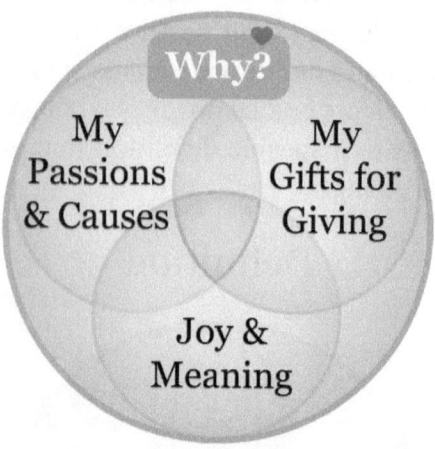

With the positive focus defined as our desire to give, to become, and to make better, the next step in the process is discovery. It is at this stage we introduce the first and most important question of all the seven essential questions for smart giving. This fundamental and core question is, "Why do we aspire to give?" (hereafter referred to as *Why?*). This question is at the root of our giving, and the answer is best elicited through our own personal storytelling by thinking about the following:

- **My Passions and Causes:** We each have moments in our lives that are significant and life-giving. It may be through the example of a parent, teacher, mentor, or coach. It may be a certain event in our life that causes us to feel alive and energized and excited. It may be a cause or passion that has attracted us through an event in our lives or through the example or experience of someone close to us. Whatever it is, there is a story behind our passion and cause and we each have personal episodes that are powerful, life-giving, energizing, and motivate us to focus our giving in a certain direction. The emotion behind our story of passion provides the answer to our *Why?* and serves as the springboard for focused, intentional and purposeful giving that brings meaning to our lives.

- **My Gifts for Giving:** In this step of the giving process, we also need to identify our core gifts for giving. What is our strength in our wheelhouse of gifts? We each have our own set of gifts for giving. It may be our unique talents, a lot of time or money on our hands, or we may be well-connected with strong relationships with many people. As with discovery of the answer to your *Why?*, we each have a story that that tells of a live-giving strength of one or more of our gifts.

- **Joy and Meaning:** With the answers to our *Why?* and the strengths found in our gifts, we will also find joy and meaning with our giving. It may be volunteering or feeling good about being able to fund a program for a cause that you are passionate about. It may be that you find great joy, meaning, and satisfaction from teaching college students or by using your trusted connections to bring resources to a cause that is important to you. Whatever the gift, the story should be joyful and meaningful to you and bring you great satisfaction.

- **Sweet spot:** The discovery step in this process reveals our deep-seated passion, our strengths, and joy and meaning. If we can find where our passions, our gifts, and joy and meaning intersect then we have found our sweet spot. Once we determine our sweet spot, we have realized what is important, life-giving and motivating to us. The sweet spot also serves as our foundation and springboard to pursue our dream of becoming a better giver and making something better that is important to us. Each of us has a sweet spot, which is visually depicted in the diagram above as the center of the three overlapping circles. For example, my wife, Suzette—a retired kindergarten teacher—finds great meaning and joy in volunteering her time at the local elementary school by helping students and teachers in any way she can. Her sweet spot is clearly the overlapping of:

- Passions and Causes—grade school students and education,
- Primary Gifts for Giving—time and talents as a former teacher, and
- Joy and Meaning—feeling good about helping both students and teachers.

Dream

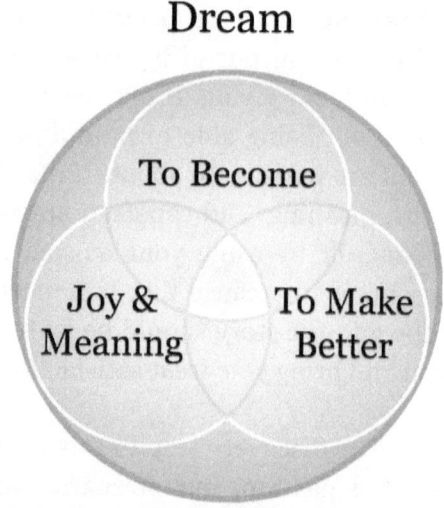

With our sweet spot identified, let's look into our crystal ball to the future. Let's envision how to use your available time, talents, trusted relationships, and financial resources. Feel and think about all the good you can do with your accumulated wheelhouse of gifts!

For if we can envision what we would like to become in service to something greater than self and we are in the position and the have the time and resources to do so, we can intentionally align and map out what we would like to become. By becoming better givers, and with a purpose that brings meaning and joy to our lives, we can then make better our small corner of the world. We can bring into a clearer focus what our future sweet spot may be.

It is this phase—the dream phase—that we think through what we would like to become, like to do, how we would like to do it, and to whom it would benefit. In the context of this philanthropic roadmap, this is not about you. This is about giving to family and causes as we become better versions of ourselves. By becoming better versions of our-selves, we are in a better position to make better a cause or situation that is important to us.

Design

Thus far we have discovered our sweet spot—the inter-section of our passions, gifts, and enjoyment—and we've also envisioned and projected what we would like to become and how we would like to use our wheelhouse of gifts. These first steps are of the giving heart, which is always the leader in our giving decisions. It is this step of the process that we introduce the concept of using seven essential questions for smart giving as a framework for the design process. Each of these questions is addressed in much more detail in chapter 6 but suffice it to say that framing the design step with these seven questions provides the Socratic methodology to ensure a thorough, comprehensive and integrated approach to the giving process. This design process includes assessing the gifts from our giving wheelhouse—our time, talent, treasure and trusted relationships, and the excess financial resources we may have.

After reviewing the answer to our "why give" question and ensuring we have aligned our purpose with our passion, we start applying our practical, rational thinking head to answer the other six questions. Some of these questions may be more emotional than others and some may be more practical. This design stage involves many philanthropic conversations and requires time for reflection and possibly additional research. I encourage you to enlist your spouse, a significant other, or some other confidant to serve as a sounding board to assure you stay true to and aligned with your *Why?* answer. You may also want to enlist the resources and guidance of professional advisors, a philanthropy coach, or a nonprofit professional.

The six questions beyond *Why?*, in no particular order, are: who to give to, what to give, when to give, where to give, how to give, and how much to give. The who we give to refers to the objects of our generosity or the beneficiaries. What to give includes the gifts of time, talents, and trusted relationships; as well as the more specific aspects of our financial resources. If we are looking at when to give financial resources, there are windows of opportunities to give throughout our life. The answer to where to give is more of a geographic question which involves tradeoffs. What to give addresses the multitude of ways we can give our financial resources, time, talents or trusted connections. One of the more nebulous questions is how much to give. Answering the question of how much to give can be easily assessed in terms of retaining life balance. With regards to our financial resources—our treasure—the determination of how much to give has not been adequately addressed for reasons to be shared later in this book. The how much to give financial question becomes much more of an emotional feeling of security than a quantitative determination.

As we transition into retirement and become accustomed to our retirement lifestyle, we normally become more concerned about financial security realizing that what we have accumulated financially is all we have. This may be especially true if we are on fixed income with no additional income sources. We may not have the security blanket of an earned income! We also realize that we must be good stewards of our life's savings and may seek out professional help to guide us in this stewardship. No one wants to outlive their money or become a burden on their children. Therefore, we put financial security first for ourselves, spouses, and families and then—from our excess—we may give to the causes and passions that are important to us. The smarter we are with our giving, the more meaningful and impactful are our gifts for giving.

Deliver

Legal Documents
& Structures

Family Love Letter

Family Letter of Intent

We have now gone through discovery clarifying our sweet spot—what is enjoyable, our gifts, what gives our lives a spark, and our passions and causes. By discovering our sweet spot, we can then envision what we would like to become and do, and how best we can contribute by transcending ourselves to better the lives of others or to serve a cause or passion greater than self. We aspire to give of our resources to become the best version of ourselves possible in service to family, others, and causes greater than self. But the three steps of discovering, dreaming and designing only serve as a foundation and stepping-stones to delivery. If we design and do not implement and deliver, we have not completed our task and fulfilled our personal mission. It is like designing your dream home and never building it! How will you deliver and how will you act upon your design? How do you "make it happen?" For if we do not deliver, we will not become, and if we do not become, we cannot do our best for our families and make better our own corner of the world; whatever that may be.

So how do we deliver? In most cases, we look to ourselves, our spouses, and other trusted relationships for feedback, counsel, and direction. Please remember that you are the captain of your ship and you must set sail and steer to your ultimate destination to "do good." Many times, we may rely on professional advisors such as our accountants, estate planning attorneys, financial advisors, and others that have the specialized expertise to answer some of our questions. The professional advisors are there for their professional counsel. YOU...with the support of your spouse, significant other, or confidant...must lead and engage your counselors and advisors to map out your giving.

Destiny

Realized Social Impact & Personal/ Family Legacy

We have taken delivery, carried out and executed our design so that we may become what we dream of. We have designed, implemented, and delivered to realize our dream. We have received immense satisfaction and meaning in our lives from reaching out by transcending ourselves to our family, to others, and to our special causes. This leads us to destiny, which refers to our legacy. Our legacy consists of two distinct kinds of legacies—a living legacy and a lasting legacy. Because we have become a better version of ourselves by transcending self while living, we are creating a living legacy that brings us great joy and satisfaction. This legacy—this life of meaning and fulfillment with intentional purpose and the aspiration to give—provides a meaningful legacy for our families, for our communities, and for future generations. Upon our death, this living legacy becomes a component of our lasting legacy.

Now as an additional note, in many cases we may think of legacy in terms of financial resources left behind, inherited by our families, charities, and others. This is a very limited perspective and for most of us our true legacy, the one that is most meaningful to us and our families, is the passing on of our non-financial assets such as our values, our life lessons, our personal and family history, the story of our lives, and our cherished memories. Our legacies—both living and lasting—are examples of a life well-lived in service to our family and something greater than self and family and serves as a shining example and a lighted pathway for others to follow. So when creating your legacy and creating your destiny, I encourage you to reach out and take the time to find those trusted resources that can help you perpetuate your values, bring meaning to your life, and help serve as an example of a life well-lived in making this world a better place.

There you have it. We've adapted the appreciative inquiry process to pioneer a new Appreciative Donor Education Process to provide a roadmap for the opportunity phase of life. Those who wish to give of their hearts from their own wheelhouse of gifts are unique and diverse. The Appreciative Donor Education Process is a donor-focused tool that can be used by individual donors, professional advisors, business owners, and nonprofit and development professionals alike. It serves as a means by which people can transition from the first half of life to a calling that is aligned, purposeful and meaningful to them. The Appreciative Donor Education Process provides the structure and framework to make the transition from the career and life you have known to the opportunities and exciting years ahead. You can now be hopeful that your future will include the opportunity to give back and make a difference. With the right resources, the right process, and the right coaches and advisors, those with a giving heart can now create their own giving future and make a difference in their world.

CHAPTER **6**

Framing Philanthropic Conversations with 7 Essential Questions

Now, you have come to that point in your life when you have checked off many of the big boxes on your personal scorecard. You are transitioning into the next phase of your life and you realize you can do more with your new-found free time and the other gifts in your wheelhouse. It is time to think about giving beyond yourself. It is liberating and exhilarating to realize you are on the precipice of an uncharted cliff—and what you do next is up to you!

Many individuals would like to learn more about family and charitable giving, but they are not sure where to begin. They want to be good stewards of their gifts and smarter with their generosity. They want to ensure that what they are giving—be it time, talent, money, or resourcing through trusted relationships—has the most impact possible.

Realize that your desire to do more for others, embracing your giving heart, and listening to your practical head are the means to an end when it comes to giving to your family or to a cause that is important to you. To begin the process, a certain amount of self-reflection and conversations with others will help you clarify your giving. Aristotle may have said it best with the following:

"To give away money is an easy matter and in any man's power. But to decide to whom to give it and how large and when, and for what purpose, is neither in every man's power nor an easy matter."

-Aristotle 360 B.C.

Aristotle's quote is focused on the giving of money, but it can also be applied to the other gifts in our giving wheelhouse. As shared in chapter 4, if our giving is to be effective, impactful, and meaningful, we should recognize and embrace the opportunity to be the best version of ourselves as philanthropists. We also need to understand the importance and need for process and the intentional alignment of our purpose with our passion. In chapter 5, we introduced the need for and derivation of the appreciative donor education process and lightly touched on seven essential questions for smart giving.

You may be wondering: why do we need the Socratic approach of using seven questions as part of this philanthropic giving process? The answer to this question is found in what is typically called the "philanthropic conversation" or, actually, conversations. You see, to arrive in a personal position where your giving is intentional, meaningful, laser-focused, and impactful, you will need to have multiple philanthropic conversations with a wide variety of people. There is a great contrast in these philanthropic conversations. Some conversations are more emotional (of the giving heart), some conversations are more rational and practical (of the thinking head), and some may engage both the heart and head. There are conversations with yourself and with others such as a spouse, significant other, or a confidant. There may be conversations with nonprofit professionals, a philanthropy coach, your minister, counselors, and other professional advisors.

Thus, the seven essential questions for smart giving provides the structure and framework for thorough, comprehensive and integrated approach to ensure our giving covers all the bases—financial and non-financial—and is smart, impactful, and personally meaningful. Hence, for smart, meaningful, and impactful giving we need:

- To lead with our Giving Heart and engage our Thinking Head,
- To seek out and engage in Giving Heart and Thinking Head philanthropic conversations, and
- Use the seven essential questions to frame your conversations to cover all the bases.

The major differences between Giving Heart and Thinking Head conversations are depicted below.

The Giving Heart

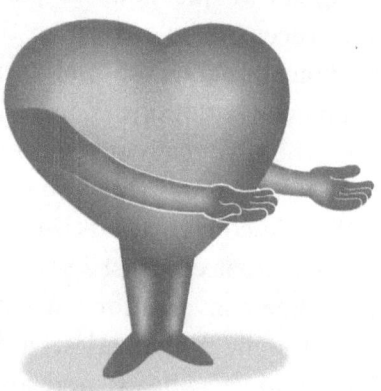

Giving Heart Conversations are primarily about "Why do I give?" and to a more limited extent "Who to give to?" and "Where should I give?"

Giving Heart Conversations are emotional conversations

about your heart, your family, your values, your causes, and your moral compass. Their roots are from your life journey, life lessons learned, schooling, events, parents, and others.

The World of the Giving Heart lives within faith traditions, spirituality, liberal arts, philosophy, counselors, psychology, sociology, and finding meaning in life.

The Thinking Head

Thinking Head Conversations are primarily about What to give?, How to give?, When to give?, and How much to give?

Thinking Head Conversations are rational, practical conversations that require thought and time, and involve logic, design, process, practicality, numbers, finances, legal documents, systems, organization, and administration.

The World of the Thinking Head lives within most professional advisors such as CPAs, bankers, financial planners, investment advisors, estate planners, and insurance agents.

The first three questions are primarily of the giving heart. These questions clarify our passion and help us align this passion with our purpose and gifts. These first of the three poignant questions start with the most important of the seven questions: "Why give?" The other two questions that reflect the object of our giving, and help us align our purpose with our passion, are "Who to give to?" and "Where to give?"

This leaves us with four remaining questions—when to give?, what to give?, how to give?, and how much to give? While these questions lead with the giving heart, they are much more down to earth and practical in terms of their application. They lean more heavily on the thinking head to find the answers. Finding the answers to these four questions often requires additional thought, planning, and possibly the professional guidance of others. This outside, trusted guidance should provide the options and possibilities available in terms of giving, especially in the giving of your financial resources (treasure). As we follow the Appreciative Donor Education Process, these remaining four questions—*When? What? How?* and *How much?*—are clearly part of the design stage of the process. But it is important to note that all seven questions are interrelated and must be considered in the context of your total giving.

We now understand that we need to have many philanthropic conversations. These varied conversations will be of an emotional and practical nature with a variety of people that may include your spouse, significant other, confidant, philanthropy coach, nonprofit professionals, and professional advisors. We also understand that we have a new tool—the seven questions—to frame our conversations to ensure we cover all the bases.

Let's dive into the discovery process and look more closely at the most important of the seven essential questions, why give?

CHAPTER 7

The Big Why?

The Answer to Meaning
and Motivation for our Giving

Of all the seven essential questions for smart giving, by far, the most important question is "why give?" This question is at the core of our giving and is all about the "heart," or the emotional reasons to give. It is the foundation on which the other six essential questions build upon. It is so vitally important that each of us dig deep within ourselves to reflect, to discover, and to understand this key to our meaning and motivation for giving.

As a clarification, we need to first understand the *Why?* in the context of our inherent nature to give. When we talk about *Why?*, we are talking about what motivates us to give to something that is greater than self. It is through our giving that we identify our purpose and it is our purpose that brings meaning to our lives. The *Why?* is not about you. It is about the free, no-strings-attached, giving of self to something beyond self; whether that be your family, your neighbors, your community, or to specific causes or passions. Often, the word self-transcendence is used to reflect this inherent need to give or reach out beyond self.

The question of *Why?* has roots in our intrinsic nature. As you may recall from chapter 2 and grade school, there is Maslow's hierarchy of needs. In researching our inherent need to give, Dr. Maslow, just before his death in 1970, addressed our innate need for self-transcendence as the highest need in The Farther Reaches of Human Nature. Dr. Maslow's understanding of this profound need to give—to transcend and to give to something greater than self—is further affirmed by Dr. Viktor Frankl, Dr. Erik Erikson, and Dr. Lars Tornstam.

Dr. Viktor Frankl was a psychiatrist, Holocaust survivor, and the founder of logotherapy, which is a model of psychotherapy based on man's motivation to search for life's meaning. His book, Man's Search for Meaning, was based on his experiences in Auschwitz, the World War II concentration camp. Subsequently, he wrote The Will to Meaning. He believed those who had meaning outside of self were driven to survive the horrors of the camp—those with a will to live and find meaning in life, even in the darkest circumstances, survived. Dr. Lars Tornstam, a Swedish sociologist and the author of Gerotranscendence: A Development Theory of Positive Aging explores our increasing self-transcendence with aging. Pulitzer Prize winner Dr. Erik Erikson in his book, The Life Cycle Completed, incorporates our need to give as reflected in the gerotranscendence of Dr. Lars Tornstam.

It is clear we have a built-in desire and need to give to something greater than ourselves. This need to give is inherent in our nature. We derive our meaning in life from our giving—our transcendence to something greater than self provides purpose and meaning and, thus, a reason to get up in the morning.

It is quite apparent that before we even think about addressing the other six essential questions for smart giving, we each need to take some time to reflect, discover, and understand our need to give and answer our own personal *Why?*. The answer to our *Why?* is unique since we are each on our one-of-a-kind life's journey and we each have different life experiences.

Realizing that understanding, defining and clarifying our *Why?* answer is the first step in the giving journey, how do we go about discovering the answer? Again, there is no right or wrong answer. For some, it may be with our own self-reflection or with help from our spouse, significant other, or confidant. For others, it may be through conversation with someone else such as a nonprofit professional or a group of peers.

We are each unique. There are real strengths in the individuality of each person; no matter what their background, no matter what their income, no matter what their life experiences, and no matter where they are in life. For you see, we are each on a life journey of aspirational giving and have been affected by our parents, teachers, mentors, coaches and other key people in our lives. We are not on this life journey alone. We have been influenced by events, causes, people, or something that has impacted us. We need to take the time to think about and identify those people, causes, or events that motivate us to give.

As a first step, I suggest you take some quiet time and reflect on three stories from your life that were impactful, shape your attitudes, and lead you to support people, events, causes, passions, institutions or something else that is meaningful to you. These three "giving motivators" helped you become what you are today and may inspire you to give to those causes or passions that are emotionally appealing, fulfilling, and bring meaning to your life.

For most of us, the first thing that comes to mind is our family. Dr. Tornstam's research reflects that mothers who have given birth are more transcendent than others. Having gone through pregnancy and given birth to their children, they fully understand what it means to give to others, to transcend self, and to dedicate one's life to the nurturing, mentoring, and growth of another. Likewise, women, in general, are more transcendent than men, and thus are typically more willing to give than men.

In conclusion, we all have an inherent need to give of ourselves to something greater than self that may include family and specific passion, community, or social causes. We have been impacted by those that have come before us. There may be teachers, parents, educators, coaches, mentors, or some other people in our lives who were influential and are the answer to our *Why?*. Maybe the answers to our *Why?* are derived from a person, event, or cause or passion. Our answer to our *Why?* will be revealed when we recognize those people and events which resonates in the very depths of our being and motivates us to make a difference in the lives of others.

In going through your discovery process to answer your *Why?* you may want to consider limiting your areas of giving to about three causes that are truly important to you. This will make it easier for you in your giving decisions and help you stay true to self, following your moral compass with aligned purpose and passion. You will also not be distracted by all the "asks" made of you. If we each answer our *Why?* and understand the reasons, then our path ahead on the common life journey of aspirational giving becomes much clearer. The answers to the *Why?* question help bring purpose, meaning, and passion to our lives. As transcendental individuals, we understand if we can pursue our purpose with passion as an answer to the *Why?* than the path on our life journey is much more defined and more meaningful. Once we have answered our *Why?* we will find that answering the other six essential questions becomes much easier.

In a nutshell...

- It is our inherent nature to give and search for a greater meaning in life through our giving.
- Answering your *Why?* is vitally important for a more meaningful and impactful life journey.
- Be patient as you reflect on the people and events to discover the answer to your *Why?*!

Chapter Exercise

The 3 main people, events, or causes that motivate me to give are:

1. Motivation:_____ Reason?_____

_____

2. Motivation:_____ Reason?_____

_____

3. Motivation:_____ Reason?_____

_____

CHAPTER 8

Who to Give to?
Finding the Beneficiaries of Your Giving

Based on your life experiences, you discovered the answer or answers to your *Why?*. This chapter is all about finding the answer to the question of who to give to (here after referred to as *Who?*). We know we have this innate, inherent desire to give of ourselves—transcend ourselves—to others, causes, or passions. As you recall from chapter 4, we also want to ensure that we intentionally align our giving. We do this to follow our own "north star" and make sure that our giving is effective and impactful. We want to ensure our gifts are making a difference to those people and to those causes that are important to us. In other words, we want to make sure that what we give —whether that be time, talents, financial resources, or our trusted connections—is going to the right organization that benefits from our generosity and that the answer to the *Who?* is intentionally aligned with the answer to our *Why?*.

You recognize you want to give. You have discovered your own individual passions and are now searching for the answer to the *Who?*. In answering this question, there are several factors to consider. The first consideration is to make sure that the category of the cause aligns with what is important to you, is congruent with your passions, and your desire to make a difference. Once you have surveyed in a broad sense, you can begin the process of narrowing down your selection. For example, let's say your personal passion is women's financial literacy. You have identified this as your own cause to champion. You believe your giving from your wheelhouse can help advance the cause and help women become more financially literate. In answering who to give to, you have identified the generic category of women's financial literacy. With this broad category outlined, you can now start narrowing down the options to answer the specifics of your *Who?*.

Let's look at some of the primary considerations in terms of your giving. Listed below are some thoughts that will help narrow and identify more specifically the answer to your *Who?*.

Transactional or Transformational Giving (or both?)

One of the primary considerations in answering your *Who?* is your desired impact of your generosity. Will your answer be of transactional or transformational benefit? What do I mean by transactional vs transformational? Transactional giving is sparked by events or situations that elicit an immediate, emotional response. These are often life events or appeals that really pull at your heart, are spontaneous with a sense of urgency, and generate an intense desire for you to give to relieve the pain, suffering, and provide immediate support of others. Examples of transactional giving are donations as a result of a natural disaster or a pull to relieve the hunger in your community. These may or may not be part of your strategic giving plan, but these gifts are worthy if it gives you a sense of meaning and fulfillment. You feel good because you are doing something—giving something—to help others. What is important is to acknowledge that these transactional gifts are driven by emotion and are important and meaningful to you.

Transformational giving is more strategic in nature. Instead of addressing more immediate needs, it is more focused on resolving the underlying reasons or causes for the situation. For a point of reference, the relationship between transactional vs. a transformational benefit may be best summarized by the familiar proverb:

"Give a man a fish, and you feed him for a day; teach a man to fish, and you feed him for a lifetime."

If you give a man a fish to solve the immediate need of hunger, you are being transactional. If you teach a man to fish, then you are being transformational in that the man knows how to feed himself and is not dependent on others. You may want to consider, broadly speaking, whether you would like to direct your giving to transactional or transformational beneficiaries. You may want to allocate a portion of your giving to both transactional and transformational beneficiaries. For example, you may want your giving to be roughly 25% transactional for the emotional, heart appealing need and 75% transformational for a more strategic, thoughtful approach. There is no right or wrong answer to the transactional or transformational allocation. Some people may be 100% transactional givers; others may be 100% transformational. What is important is that your giving is intentionally aligned and allocated to what is important and meaningful to you.

The Nonprofit's Mission

A critical consideration in answering your *Who?* is to closely review and ensure the mission of the organization and the work it performs is aligned with your passion, your purpose, and your *Why?* answer. Take a step back and review your answer to *Why?* and see if the answer to your *Who?* is congruent and makes sense. To confirm that you feel good about an organization you may want to schedule an on-site visit to become fully aware of the work that they are doing. Ask a lot of questions and look for transparency, conditions, attitudes, and how people interact (or not) with you. An on-site visit also provides the opportunity to gain a sense of how you feel about giving to the organization and if you are comfortable that the organization is fulfilling its mission.

Small, medium, or large organization?

Another consideration is the size of the organization. Frequently, small local nonprofits have a tremendous passion for their mission. They have an immense, giving heart and honestly believe in the cause. However, small community nonprofits, in many cases, do not have the experience, skills, processes, and infrastructure for long-term sustainability. Larger organizations, on the other hand, have been around longer and may have local branches in different communities. While larger organizations may have the tools, processes, structure, and experience in dealing with donors (including financial donations), the national organizations may not be as flexible in working with you as a donor and may allocate part of their financial donations (including your gift) to the national organization.

A Relationship

Often, we may have a personal, professional, or community relationship with someone in a nonprofit that is appealing to us and appears to be an easy answer to our *Who?*.

Without much thought, it makes it simple to answer our *Who?*. Many people give to nonprofits based on someone they know affiliated with the organization and with whom they have a relationship. Many giving hearts who give in this way may not have taken the time to go through their own discovery process to identify their unique passions and causes. Personal giving may become a primary action of obligation and loyalty to someone else and not as a result of aligning your personal and the organization's mission.

Nonprofit Metrics

It is time to engage your thinking head in terms of the parameters and impact of the nonprofit you are considering giving to. Usually, the availability and the use of metrics by nonprofits is not part of their DNA—their makeup in fulfilling their mission. This is especially true for smaller, local nonprofits. After all, nonprofits are typically founded on emotion—the giving heart—and those emotional connections are the motivation for people to give from their wheelhouse. With this said, metrics are essential. For example, is the nonprofit financially self-sustaining, or are they continually asking for money? What is their plan for generating sustainable financial funding—funding that is consistent and predictable? What percentage of their funding comes from grants? Sponsorships? Self-generating revenues?

On the expense side of the ledger, a well-established nonprofit would have three major categories of expenses as follows:

- **Overhead** is the normal operating expenses of the nonprofit and includes salaries, utilities, rent and all the expenses to just stay in the nonprofit business.

- **Capacity Building** are expenses that are invested in the nonprofit so they can grow and improve its ability to meet its mission in the future.

- **Program expenses** are those expenditures generated from carrying out the nonprofit's mission. For example, in the case of financial literacy, such expenses would be the cost of educational symposiums to improve women's financial literacy.

On the expense side, what percent of expenses are overhead and capacity building? What percentage of funding is spent on programs to meet the nonprofit's mission? If there is too much overhead and capacity building, then the mission may be slighted. Therefore, it is vital to understand the allocation of expenses of overhead vs. capacity building vs. mission-focused programs. You as a giving heart, need to understand and be comfortable with the breakdown of the allocation of expenses. It is most certainly worth asking the question: what is the allocation of funding to overhead vs. capacity building vs. mission program expenses?

While nonprofits often do not have a financial return on investment, one metric that is becoming increasingly important for donors is social return on investment (SROI). Numerous philanthropic research studies reveal that donors are searching for personal meaning from their giving and that their donation have a direct beneficial impact. Donors, especially those with a business or financial background, are increasingly wanting to see the impact of their financial giving. How does the nonprofit measure and benchmark their progress in meeting their mission and achieving their goals? The SROI for nonprofits is analogous to the financial return on investment (ROI) that is commonplace in business. Unlike the financial ROI, which is purely mathematical, SROI is much harder to determine since it is dependent on hard-to-measure results.

Let's be realistic. For small financial donations to non-profits, assessing the SROI for a gift is not feasible. Smaller organizations typically do not have the time, processes, or other resources to determine a measured social return. Hence, with smaller gifts, there is a lesser focus on quantifying the measured impact of giving or, more specifically, of quantifying the social return on investment. The greater the financial donation, the more it is expected that the benefitting nonprofit can and should provide a SROI. If a measurable SROI is important to you it is worth asking questions such as:

- What is your SROI?
- How is your SROI derived?
- What is your nonprofit's SROI history?

Whether or not a nonprofit can provide a SROI to prospective donors can be very telling and can be used as a factor in determining who you may want to give to.

In summary, there are a number of considerations in answering your *Who?*. Please see the diagram to the right that depicts the considerations in answering *Who?*. Do you want your giving to be transactional, transformational, or both? Is the nonprofit fulfilling its mission? Do you have a personal connection to the nonprofit? Have you assessed the pros and cons the nonprofits size and reviewed its metrics (if available)?

Thus far, we have fully engaged our giving hearts in identifying those passions, causes, or events in our lives that had an impact, and motivate us to give to others, transcend, and to serve something greater than self. We answered the question of *Why?*. We have then been able to take our passions and align them with the recipient of our generous hearts, discovering the answer to *Who?*. Realizing that we all want to make an impact and know we are making an impact with our generosity, we looked at various considerations to further clarify and identify the recipients of our giving. To be impactful and derive more meaning from our generosity, it is essential to understand and engage our thinking head as part of the process for aligning the answers of *Who?* and *Why?*.

There are a lot of considerations. There are resources available, which may include various online resources to help you better understand who the best beneficiary for your intentional, smart giving is. Also, there are resources such as philanthropy coaches and personal and professional relationships. Local community foundations serve as an excellent source to help you align your passion, purpose, and match your giving in the community.

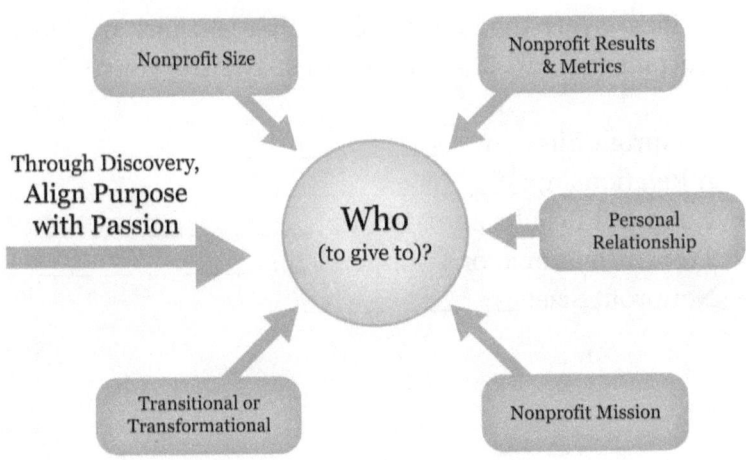

In a nutshell...

- Answering Why? will point you to the broad categorical answer to your *Who?*.
- Engage your thinking head to identify organizational considerations for *Who?*.
- Do your homework, ask questions, and spend time with potential organizations.
- Don't be afraid to ask for help. Discuss with your family and friends and seek out your local community foundation for guidance.
- Take the time to make sure the answers to your Why? and *Who?* are aligned.

Chapter Exercise

Through discovery, you have discovered your passions or causes that are meaningful and important to you. Please rate the factors below that you feel are most important (1 = Most, 5 = Least) in answering your *Who?*:

- Nonprofit Mission:_____
- A Relationship:_____
- Nonprofit Results and Metrics:_____
- Transformational or Transactional: _____
- Nonprofit Size: _____

CHAPTER 9

Where to Give?

Assessing Tradeoffs
of our Wheelhouse Gifts

Before we begin addressing the where to give question (here after referred to as *Where?*), let's clearly define what we mean by where. *Where?* is all about geographical location of the benefits of your generosity. It may be your hometown, your region, country or some foreign third-world country. If you take a moment to consider and think about the geographic location of the receiving organization you are considering for your generosity, there are tradeoffs involved with regards to our giving wheelhouse. These tradeoffs...the pros and cons...should at least be recognized as part of the giving process.

Let's take a take a moment and review the questions we have addressed so far. The *Why?* is by far the most critical question of the seven. It is the bedrock that serves as the foundation from which we determine the answers to the other six questions.

Being intentional and purposeful with our giving results in greater joy, meaning, and impact. Our giving brings more personal fulfillment when we take the time to think about it and carefully make a realistic action plan. Like so many other transactional choices in our fast-paced, media-driven, live day-by-day world, we react and emotionally respond to something at that moment. We become transactional givers by spontaneously acting because it is quick, easy, and immediate. As we each reflect on our life journey and we take a moment to identify our passions and causes—answers to our *Why?*—and then broadly identify the answer to *Who?* we have made a significant leap in the giving journey and established the framework for answering the other five essential questions. Shown below is the sequence in clarifying our answers to the *Why?*, *Who?*, and *Where?*:

Why?→*Who? (Category)*→*Where?*→*Who?(Specific)*

Once we discover the answer to our *Why?*, we find out, in a generic sense, the answer to *Who?*. Once we have broadly identified the answer to *Who?*, we need to take a slight detour on our philanthropic giving journey to find the answer to *Where?*. By detouring and obtaining clarity on our answer to *Where?*, we can then re-focus on identifying the direct beneficiary that is the answer to *Who?*.

By intentionally aligning our purpose with our passion, we are emotionally congruent and have discovered our *Why?* answer, and in a general sense, our *Who?* answer. Our next step is to look at the options for our *Where?*. We will be able to assess these options in light of our own giving wheelhouse of time, talents, treasure, and trusted relationships. From there, we can resume pinpointing our specific *Who?*. What role does *Where?* have in helping us align our *Why?* and *Who?* and what are the considerations?

Since this all may sound confusing, I will simplify through a real-life example. Let's continue with women's financial literacy as our cause. Having identified it as the answer to our *Why?*, you may know first-hand or through a dear friend or relative the pain of not being financially literate. Broadly speaking, you want to do your part to help women become financially literate. It is a cause that your deeply believe in and want to help through your giving. Hence, the broad categorical answer to *Who?* is aligned to your answer to *Why?* To assure we are thorough, we should consider our *Where?*. In other words, where geographically do we want to make an impact and help women become financially literate? Is it in a third world country or international in scope? Are we talking about women's financial literacy in our own country? Our own region? Our own hometown? Within a specific local community like a women's club or university?

Once the broad aspect of *Who?* is answered, the next step in this sequence is to look at the tradeoffs involved in our giving. Let's look at the tradeoffs and how geographic distance may have on the gifts from our giving wheelhouse. Once you have realized the strength of your gifts, you may want to consider which gift would make the greatest impact. For some, their primary offering in their wheelhouse is time. While others may not have time but may have excess financial resources. It may be easiest to break down each category of giving and assess the strengths you have to offer and what makes the most giving sense to you.

Time: Most of us consider the gift of our time as being extremely important in seeking the answer to *Where?*. The greater the geographic distance, the more time it would take you to travel which reduces the time for impact or pursue other priorities such as family. Also, time spent traveling is neither transactional nor transformative; it is just spent time. If you decide to provide locally and it is a viable option, the gift of time is less affected by travel and provides more flexibility. If the giving goal you wish to achieve is through the efficient use of your gift of time, then the *Where?* answer may be closer to home with less travel.

Talents: In the discovery phase of this philanthropic giving process, we identified the talents, skills, life lessons, and wisdom we have accumulated. We now have these talents to offer and we **find meaning through our** gifting of these talents. In continuing with the example of women's financial literacy as the answer to our *Who?*, our talents may not be relevant if we are considering gifting to third world countries. There are other higher priorities than financial literacy in third world countries. In this instance of women's financial literacy, for example, it may make much more sense to bring your talents to promote women's financial literacy in a more developed nation where there is a bigger need for your talents.

Treasure: Often, the generous giving of our financial resources is emotionally appealing. Maybe a promotion to sponsor a child either domestically or internationally tugged at your heart strings and prompted a donation. Perhaps you have a soft spot for neglected animals and saw a way to make a one-time donation to a rescue organization. Frequently our financial generosity is an impromptu decision that is emotionally appealing, easy, and quick. That is okay. What IS important is that you recognize these heart-pulling appeals as they are. They are intentional, emotional appeals to your giving heart. Generally, the more you give financially, the more due diligence should be performed as a steward of your financial resources. Likewise, the greater the financial gift, the more important it becomes to assure your gift has the desired impact.

For small financial donations, you are hoping and trusting that they are handling your donation with sound stewardship. In addition, please be aware that more financial due diligence is needed for international giving due to the increased risks involved. If you are considering donating outside the United States, it makes sense to find specialists in global charitable giving that can help you better understand the risks, obstacles, and capabilities of those organizations that provide international services.

Trust: As stated previously, our trusted relationships with others is a great resource and is oftentimes overlooked as a gift. So how do our trusted relationships impact the *Where?* For most of us, our trusted relationships are local. With that said, if we assess our accumulated relationships and find that some of our relationships include a regional, national, or international connection, then we may want to consider reaching out to this trusted resource as part of our giving process. Who knows, an outside trusted relationship may have their own wheelhouse of gifts that can help you and your cause. If we do not have these outside trusted relationships in our giving wheelhouse, then we need to recognize and understand the limitation of our trusted relationships.

In a nutshell...

- We need the broad, categorical answer to *Who?* before answering our *Where?*
- There are time and money cost considerations in the answering our *Where?*
- The answer to *Where?* helps us find our specific answer to our *Who?*

Chapter Exercise:

1. The answer to my *Why?* is:_____
2. The broad categorical answer to my *Who?* is:_____

_____

3. After considering my wheelhouse of gifts and the answers to my *Why?* and categorical *Who?*, my answer to *Where?* is: _____

_____

_____

CHAPTER **10**

When to Give?

Timing is Very Important to Magnify Meaning and Impact

As you may recall, our common life journey of aspirational giving is divided into three main phases: accumulation, opportunity, and distribution. In the accumulation phase, we are gathering and building personal relationships, amassing financial resources, fine-tuning our skills, learning from work experiences, and continually learning from our unique life experiences. The second phase is the opportunity phase, which provides a prime window of opportunity for us to give from our amassed gifts along with our new time-freedom and the flexibility time-freedom brings. Lastly, there is the distribution phase which has its own opportunities for giving.

We clearly understand that we each have our own unique gifts of time, talents, financial resources, and trusted relationships. No matter what stage of life we are in— the accumulation, opportunity, or distribution phase—we each need to take time to reflect on this next question of the seven essential questions on when we should give (here after referred to *When?*).

For many, the answer to the *When?* is straightforward. After assessing our situation on our life journey and answering our *Why?*, *Who?*, and *Where?*, the decision to give of time, talents, and trusted relationships should be fairly straightforward and easy since the answer to *When?* is simply a scheduling issue. The answer to the *When?* for our giving of money may be more challenging. Money is real, tangible, and highly personal. We may have a unique relationship with money based on our life experience. Typically, we use money in our daily living and money is a constant presence in our lives; either through its use or through the media. There always seems to be people, nonprofits, and other causes asking for our money—a donation to help this or that cause. Can we donate to this or financially support that? Many times, the requests are emotionally appealing, and we give without much thought. Because money (or the lack of it) is so present and relevant to our daily living, let me share with you my experience in helping clients financially prepare for, transition into, and navigate retirement or the next phase of their life. This will help in answering *When?*. Let's start by looking at the concept of "money in motion."

Money in motion

In the early part of my career guiding clients into and through retirement, I came across the concept of money-in-motion. What do I mean by money in motion? In its most straightforward context, money in motion refers to those disruptive events—life transitions—that cause us to review and make changes in our financial lives. The life event is such that there is a need for us to transfer, consolidate, sell, buy, distribute, exchange, gift, or re-title financial assets.

Money is in motion when life goes into transition.

During most of our life journey, our personal financial lives are on cruise control—we save, spend, and invest on a routine basis (hopefully, consistent with our financial plan!). Our financial situation is systematic and constant; maybe even boring! This financial status quo provides us with a sense of predictability, routine, calmness, and (hopefully!) a feeling of current and future financial security.

The Life Journey of Aspirational Giving

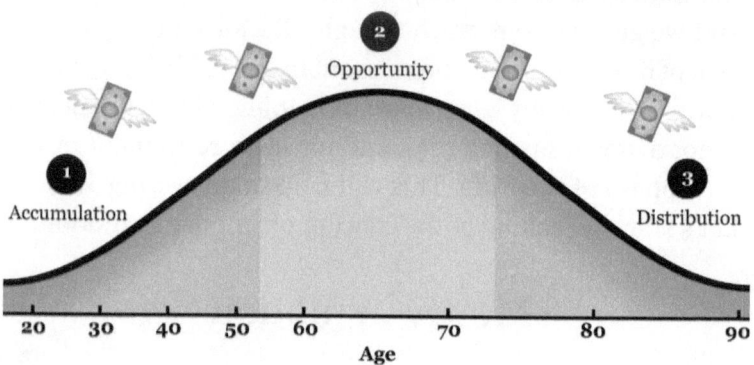

But as we all know, our life journey is not one continuous path that remains the same. As we continue to travel on our road of life, we encounter occasional, sometimes disruptive events that change the trajectory and routine of our lives. Listed below are a few examples of life events that may lead to money in motion:

- College graduation
- Marriage
- Divorce
- Job or Career Change
- Retirement
- Relocation
- Business Sale/Purchase
- Disability
- Age 70 ½
- Death

These life events cause us to review our personal finances and typically result in money in motion. It is during these times that we become more anxious, insecure about our future, and want to make smart, informed decisions. We may seek out professional guidance. It is these kinds of life events when there is an opportunity for money in motion in terms of ownership, custody, transference, or some other movement of our money. As we approach, enter, and navigate the opportunity phase, there are money in motion events such as retirement, the sale of a business, age 70 ½, and death of a spouse or parent. These all become potential opportunities for meaningful and impactful financial giving. Depending on the circumstances, anticipating transitions should be viewed as a possible opportunity to make tax-smart giving decisions to your family and those causes that are important to you.

By understanding the concept of money in motion, we can look to answer *When?* by reviewing our own life journey—starting with the accumulation phase.

During the accumulation phase, we are saving for retirement, acquiring our talents in the form of experiences, skills, and education, and building networks of personal, professional, and community relationships. Time is at a premium during this phase as we are busy with building a career and maybe raising a family. If we are giving—donating—during the accumulation phase, our donations are typically of time and money and we do so in the form of a routine, allocated amount of both time and of money.

Within our giving wheelhouse, we may be limited by our resources of time and treasure. If we are fortunate enough to have a surplus of income or savings above and beyond any that may be needed for financial and family security, we may have an opportunity to give in a smart and impactful manner. As with most people in the accumulation phase, the higher earners typically may not have the time or the know-how on how best to gift excess income or financial resources. If high-income earners during the accumulation phase have the means and want to give beyond their own personal and family financial needs, they may want to seek guidance from trusted advisors.

The second phase of our life journey is the opportunity phase. It provides many with prime-life opportunities to look deep within their being and give from the heart to make a difference, gain more meaning to life, and create both a living and lasting legacy. You have spent a lifetime of accumulating in the form of building a career, maybe raising a family, establishing trusted relationships, gaining professional and life skills and talents, and spending and investing for savings, real estate, or a successful business. As we approach this giving opportunity phase, we also realize we will have a lot more time to spend with family and friends, travel, or pursuing other interests to include volunteering. What a sense of freedom—to have time to do all the things we have dreamed of doing! Time—that elusive friend during the accumulation phase—is now at the forefront. For those of you with a giving heart, why not use all your accumulated gifts to do good? For those wishing to find their post-career and post-family raising purpose in life, it is time to find and align your new purpose with your passions, talents, treasure, and trusted relationships.

The opportunity phase is typically recognized in midlife and it becomes a very real and personal when you begin to plan for anticipate the next phase of life. Typically, with new time-freedom, the opportunity phase provides those with a giving heart the opportunity to give from their accumulated talents, skills, education, financial resources, and the trusted relationships. The freedom to schedule your time and spend it on what is important to you is the highlight of retirement and the opportunity phase. I suggest you begin to envision and plan for your transition at least five to seven years before your retirement date. The answer to *When?* in the opportunity phase is the transition from a time of family-raising and a career to a new calling. It is the prime time in life to find a new reason to get up in the morning and find a new purpose with meaning.

Throughout our life journey we have each developed skills and talents, accumulated financial resources, and built years of trusted relationships through personal and professional networks. As we enter the opportunity phase, we anticipate the time we will be able to give more freely and to make an intentional direct impact. This in turn, brings additional personal meaning to our lives.

Many times, during the opportunity phase, people look to simplify their lives. This is a time to clean out your "financial attic." This may include combining financial accounts, selling business interests or real estate that is becoming more difficult and complex to retain and maintain. It may become easier to distribute the property either by selling, gifting or by some other means. This inclination to simplify one's life serves as a prompt to ask the question, "Is this a good time to explore how I can simplify my life and do social good at the same time?" Once again, it becomes an opportunity to answer the question, "When do I give?"

To accomplish this goal of smart giving during the opportunity phase, let's look at all of the gifts you gathered during the accumulation phase. You now have the chance make a real difference with your giving. In the opportunity phase, decisions must be made as to how much you will give of your time to family and those causes or passions that are important to you. Likewise, it is also an opportunity to give of your accumulated talents in education, professional skills, and accumulated life experiences. Furthermore, it is an opportunity to bring those trusted relationships to the causes and passions that are important to you. Financially, as you transition into and throughout the early retirement years, you will be adjusting your monthly cash flow and firming up your spending plan. You also realize that your career of earning a living may be ending and you will be living on a fixed income, so there may be some financial insecurities.

If during the opportunity phase, you find yourself with more-than-needed financial resources for your personal and family economic security, then it may prove to be an excellent time to align the giving of your time, your talents, your relationships, and excess financial resources with those causes that are really important to you. By aligning your own giving gifts, this may be an extremely fulfilling and meaningful time and be an answer to your *When?*.

Let's move on past the opportunity phase to the distribution phase. It is during the distribution phase that we reflect upon our personal legacy. It is during this time that we have settled into a routine retirement lifestyle. We may have enough, and possibly excess, financial resources from which we want to give. One of the primary questions during this distribution phase is whether you should give while you are living or bequest it upon your death? If you give while living, you will have more control over how the gifts are directed, reap the emotional rewards of your generosity, and intentionally craft and live your personal legacy. Or, do you feel the need to retain your financial resources to ensure the financial security of your family, or to support them in their pursuits on their life journey of aspirational giving? These are just a few examples of the things to consider.

There are also times during the distribution phase when there are life events that provide opportunities for smart giving to family and the causes that are important to you.

Multi-generational family vacations, for example, provide an ideal time for generating memories and the sharing of values. Financial gifting to children or grandchildren for specific needs such as college or down payment on a new home are also very meaningful. Financially, when you reach the age of 70 ½, the IRS requires individuals to take a required minimum distribution (RMD) from their retirement and IRA accounts (except for Roth IRAs). This required distribution is an opportunity for those older than age 70 ½ to make a qualified charitable distribution (QCD) to qualified nonprofit 501c (3) organizations. Depending on your financial situation, a QCD may provide tax advantages if these funds are not needed for routine living expenses or financial security.

Lastly, during the distribution phase, you have the opportunity to craft your legacy through conversations, documentation, letters to your family, and personal and family archiving. All of these are gifts of love to your family and help answer your *When?*. Whether it be a bequest through your will, a trust document, or through the designated contractual beneficiary designation such as IRAs or life insurance policies, the distribution phase becomes an excellent opportunity to leave a lasting impact beyond one's lifetime to family and those causes that are important and meaningful. It is highly recommended that you seek out the wisdom of your spouse, significant other, confidant, and professional advisors. If your financial resources are in excess, it may be worthwhile to engage a philanthropy coach to serve as your quarterback in collaboration with your other professional advisors.

There you have it! In summary, we each have our own giving wheelhouse of time, talents, financial resources, and trusted relationships. Our wheelhouse accumulates financial resources, trusted personal relationships, and education, career skills, and life experience during the accumulation phase.

Unless we have excess resources, during the accumulation phase the *When?* answer is of low priority considering the busyness of life. The accumulation phase transitions into the opportunity phase, which is the peak time for giving and provides numerous opportunities to answer *When?*.

The distribution phase of our life journey is another prime time to answer *When?* These may include the distribution of retirement plan assets and the legacy creation of both non-financial assets and financial assets upon our passing. All three of these phases—the accumulation, the opportunity, and the distribution—are each punctuated by life events that trigger money in motion and may spark the question of, "Is this the time when I can give to make a difference, make a positive impact, and bring more meaning to my life?"

As a final thought, the *When?* is just one of the seven essential questions for smart giving. The answer to this particular question during our life journey is intertwined with the other six questions and may prompt the need for additional thought, conversation, and in some cases, professional guidance.

In a nutshell...

- For most people, the answer to *When?* generally has the lowest impact and priority during the accumulation phase.
- As you review your own position on your life journey of aspirational giving and seek the answer to *When?*, you need to assess two factors—Where are you on life's journey?... and...When do you foresee your money will be in motion?
- It's important to recognize those money-in-motion moments as potential giving opportunities that may answer *When?*.

Chapter Exercise:

1. What phase of the life journey are you in?_____

_____

2. My money was "in motion" when:_____

_____

3. I see the following money in motion times in the years
   ahead:_____

_____

4. Upon reflection, what is the most opportune answer to
   my *When?* for the gift of:
   - Time:_____
   - Treasure:_____
   - Talents:_____
   - Trusted Relationships:_____

CHAPTER 11

What to Give?

Since we can't take it with us, let's give wisely now and later

As we proceed through this giving process, we have now uncovered the answer to *Why?*. Now, we are in the midst of the design phase of the giving process. We have found the object of our giving by answering *Who?* and *Where?* and started assessing the more practical answer to *When?*.

This chapter addresses the considerations in answering another pragmatic question—what should we give? (here after referred to as *What?*). In seeking the answer to the pragmatic *What?* we need to take an inventory of our gifts. Do we have more time than money? Do we have networks of trusted relationships that we may be able to call on? What do we have amongst our gifts that brings the most impact and most meaning to us individually?

With this said, we cannot lose sight of the primary importance of our motivation for purposeful giving to make better the causes and passions that are important to us, bring meaning to our lives, and make this world a better place. In consideration of our unique gifts of giving, let's take a closer look at each of the four gifts in seeking the answer to our *What?*.

Time: As you may recall from our common life journey of aspirational giving, during the accumulation phase, we do not have the time to do much other than to spend and invest our time in ourselves, our families, our careers, and other routine day-to-day activities.

During the opportunity stage of life, one of the biggest challenges many people face during their retirement transition are finding the answers to the questions, "What is my purpose for getting up in the morning? What will be the structure of my day? And how will I be engaging others?" For those with a giving heart, this provides the opportunity to engage people in a meaningful and impactful way that is consistent and aligned with the causes and passions that are important to them.

With time-freedom and flexibility of the opportunity phase, there are many meaningful and impactful volunteer opportunities to give either by spending (transactional) time or investing (transformational) time in ways that can bring joy, meaning, and fulfillment to you.

Talents: Throughout one's lifetime, one accumulates extensive talents. By the time you reach the age that you transition into retirement, everyone, no matter what their background, has gained a lifetime of experience, skills, education, and life lessons learned. This accumulation of talents is part of everyone's giving wheelhouse. As you may recall from the discovery phase, it is at this time that we reflect and recognize our own unique talents. We recognize that we can give of these talents so they are intentionally aligned and congruent; thus, answering the *Why?*, *Who?*, and *Where?*.

Let's look at our example of women's financial literacy. In the discovery process, we discovered the desire to serve and advocate for women's financial literacy. If our education, talents, skills, and experience can advance that mission to improve women's financial literacy, then it becomes more meaningful and has the most potential impact.

Treasure: Although it is only one of the four gifts, it is oftentimes the top of mind answer when people first think about philanthropic giving. If we are so fortunate as to have excess financial resources, we should serve as good stewards and examples of philanthropic generosity. With sound stewardship and intentional, thoughtful, and aligned giving, we can achieve more meaning and make a greater impact to benefit those causes that are important to us.

For those with abundant financial resources that would like to give from their surplus to family and their special causes, there may be some additional complexities and challenges to address. Within one's financial portfolio, there are different types of financial assets and additional guidance may be needed from a coach or professional advisors to clarify the answer to *What?*. Generally speaking, the greater the financial resources available for giving, the more complex smart giving becomes, and the more need for personal reflection, conversation, evaluation of options, and the need for professional guidance.

For example, if someone is wealthy, they may review their own portfolio for different assets that may be suitable for giving. Appreciated stocks, real estate of all kinds, a privately held business, or some collectibles may be some of the assets suitable for gifting. This is also the time to take a pragmatic approach and seek collaborative professional guidance to find the best answer to *What?*. In addition, if the gift is significant and more complex, a comprehensive approach may be needed to evaluate the options and integrate the answer to *What?* with the answers to *When?*, *How?*, and *How much?*.

Trust: By far, the most overlooked gift we have in our giving wheelhouse is our trusted relationships with others. As we approach, transition into, and enjoy our time in the opportunity phase, we need to recognize that we have accumulated a lifetime of trusted relationships with others. If we take time for reflection, we may have trusted relationships that can bring additional value and benefit to the cause or passion that is important to us. After all, we have developed these relationships and bonded on a personal or professional level for 30 years or more. Hopefully, we retained some of these key relationships and can engage them as needed. In answering *What?* these personal and professional relationships may have far more potential than we first realize. If we engage these trusted resources, we may be able to leverage and significantly amplify the impact of our own aligned and intentional giving by bringing other resources to the table.

For example, let's go back to our cause of women's financial literacy. We have been generous with our time. We have been generous with our talents and may have even provided leadership to advance women's financial literacy. We have also given of our financial resources, but we have overlooked the influence and the impact of our own trusted relationships.

Let's say you have a trusting relationship with someone who is not familiar with the women's financial literacy organization you choose to support. You also recognize that this trusting relationship has some specific knowledge on a financial literacy topic that she could share. You realize that, because of your relationship, you can ask this resource to share her knowledge with your group. Who knows, she may even provide some provide additional financial funding too! All it may take from you is the simple recognition of the potential impact of the trusting relationship and then a willingness to ask if she would be willing to share her knowledge.

In a nutshell...

- In answering the question *What?*, we need to take a full inventory of our four gifts—time, talent, treasure and trust.
- Are we rich in time? Are we rich in the talents we can bring? Are we richer in the financial resources we can provide? Or, are we rich in the relationships we can bring that we can leverage and amplify the impact of all the other gifts we have to offer?
- It is highly probable that we can bring to the table a combination of all our gifts that provide optimal and impactful giving.

End of Chapter Exercise:

In answering *What?* my gifts of giving that will bring the most meaning and have the greatest impact on the causes that are important to me, in order are:

1. _____
   _____
2. _____
   _____
3. _____
   _____
4. _____
   _____

CHAPTER 12

The How?

The Tools and Techniques
of the Education Process

We have thus far answered the first three questions that align our purpose and passion and clarify the object of our mission. We know the answers to our *Why?*, *Who?*, and *Where?*. The how-to-give question (here after referred to as *How?*) is a down-to-earth, practical question that is interrelated with the other design questions of *When?*, *What?*, and *How much?*. Like all of the seven essential questions, *How?* is another framing question to help make smart giving decisions. Finding the answer to *How?* is addressed in the design phase of the appreciative donor education process.

The answer to the *How?* question normally comes to the forefront in the opportunity and distribution phases of our life journey. It is at this time in our lives when we have accumulated our numerous talents, amassed (hopefully!) sufficient financial savings, and have developed and retained trusted personal and professional relationships. Throughout the years, we have hopefully become wiser from life and work lessons-learned, and we realize that we have an increased motivation to make a difference and give back to something greater than self. We are at a time in our lives when we can focus on how to give to our families and to give back to better our world for those that will follow us. Depending on our personal situation, we may want to leverage the opportunity to give as we transition into retirement. Let's look more specifically at each of our wheelhouse gifts to uncover answers to *How?*.

Time: One of the most significant changes in transitioning from the accumulation phase to the opportunity phase is the awareness of the new time-freedom you will have once you are retired. While you were working, maybe you had a daily routine that was structured for eight hours per day within a five-day work week. Now you will be able to spend your time doing what you want when you want! This feeling of time-freedom provides us with a sense of new independence and time flexibility. While this time-freedom is exciting and provides us with the opportunity to find new purpose and meaning in our lives, it also may be a little unnerving as you face the prospect of no defined structured in a daily routine.

In looking at how we use our time to transcend self and family, most people think of the giving of their time in a volunteer capacity. Volunteering is the most routine and typical way people give of their time. This may be the initial thought and easiest answer to *How?*. As an initial impulse, we may reach out to volunteer with some organization that is emotionally appealing which may...or may not... be aligned with our defined purpose and the answer to our *Why?*. To dig deeper, let's take a closer look at volunteering your time to ask a more clarifying question on the type of volunteering. Is your gifting of time as a volunteer *transactional* or *transformational*? Is the difference important to you? Do you know the difference? An example of a *transactional* gifting of time is volunteering at a local food bank or a hospital to relieve or address an immediate need. Or, would you like to be intentional and invest your time to transform an existing situation that betters lives, the environment, or your community?

Both transactional and transformational giving is needed. What is important to note is that to be a smart giver, you need to recognize whether your giving is transactional or transformational, and that ultimately, that you feel good and achieve meaning from your giving.

In allocating your time in this opportunity phase of life, how much effort do you make to align your time with the cause or passion that is meaningful to you? How do you do this? Are you spending your time in a transactional way? The use of our precious time can take multiple forms. For example, it can be as simple as investing your time in helping students learn to read. Or it may be investing your time in a social enterprise or in personal self-development so that your own giving impact has a more significant societal benefit and brings meaning to you.

Talents: As we near the end of the accumulation phase and approach and transition into the next phase of life, we may have spent 30- or 40-years gaining life and career experiences. We may have accumulated knowledge and hopefully, wisdom, by living, working, playing, raising a family, learning professional skills and acquiring an education, and learning many lessons—sometimes the hard way!

All our living experiences are collected in our warehouse of talents. It is part of the broader wheelhouse of gifts that we each carry with us. It would be a waste to see all these talents be put on a shelf or go to waste! In the years ahead, how may your abilities be used? How can you bring the very best of all your life skills, experience, wisdom, and knowledge to the table to help causes that are truly important to you and how will you answer your *How?*. How can you do this in a way that is meaningful, impactful, and measurable? As you may recall, during the discovery phase of the giving process, you identified your sweet spot, which is the overlapping of your unique gifts, passions, and what you found meaningful. This may be the time to reflect on those tremendous talents you have accumulated and apply them to make a difference.

Treasure: Next up in the four giving gifts is our gift of financial resources, money, or treasure. Answering the *How?* as it applies to our money requires the engagement of our thinking head—not just the giving heart. If you have a limited spending plan, the giving of your financial resources may take the form of stewardship giving—the routine giving of a set amount each month to the cause or passion that matters to you. If you are fortunate enough to have excess resources beyond what is needed for your family's financial security, you may want to consider supplemental giving that is explicitly tied to the specific benefit or impact of the object of your giving.

The philanthropic sector is evolving and introducing new ways of giving which supplement traditional charitable tools and techniques. Today, financial giving has taken on new forms. In terms of leading-edge philanthropic giving, there are relatively new ways to give financially via crowdfunding, mobile gifting, and other gifting platforms. These new giving options provide even those with limited financial resources easy and quick means to give. They also demonstrate that no matter the level of giving, some thoughtful care should be given to your *How?*. With an inherent need to give, and to utilize both the traditional and newer forms of giving, many are wanting to learn more about their options on how to give effectively and wisely.

For those with more modest financial means, the answer to *How?* may be as simple as the now somewhat old-fashioned practice of writing a check, gifting appreciated investment securities, or—for those older than age 70 ½—making a qualified charitable distribution (QCD) from an IRA. In addition, other techniques, such as crowdfunding, pooled income funds, giving circles, donor advised (DAF) funds, and charitable gift annuities may be options to answer your *How?*.

If you are fortunate enough to have excess financial resources, the answer to *How?* may become more complex and challenging. Those with a higher net worth or income may have financial assets such as business interests, a second-home, rental property, commercial real estate, appreciated stocks, a successful professional practice, a large balance in retirement accounts such as IRAs or 401(K), or even collectibles.

With a higher net worth or income, there are more options that require additional conversations to answer your *How?* for smart, meaningful, and tax-efficient gifting. In these cases, the approach to answer *How?* needs to be methodical, thorough, and integrated with the answers to *What?*, *When?*, and *How much?*. This will require additional planning and thoughtful consideration. Those of a more modest financial means may want to find their answers through personal assessment and research.

For those with excess financial resources, there are giving vehicles, tools, and techniques that may answer your *How?*. These may be used as stand-alone, or in some cases, combined with other options. These tools and techniques may include private foundations, charitable remainder and charitable lead trusts (each with their own options!), donor advised funds (DAF), social impact investing, qualified charitable distributions (QCD), beneficiary designations, disclaimers, life estates, charitable gift annuities, gifting of appreciated stock and property, the smart use of insurance, and other tools and techniques. It can certainly be overwhelming! In these cases, you may want to engage a philanthropy coach to collaborate with your professional advisors for a team-based approach to identify your best options on how to give. By following the appreciative donor education process in a deliberate and thoughtful manner, these more complex and large financial giving situations typically take time. For the best results, allow yourself time for a series of meetings, personal processing, and additional research. And, of course, this team is led and directed by you!

Trust: This all too often overlooked gift in our giving wheelhouse is one of the most important resources we have but is rarely discussed in the philanthropic context. No man is an island unto himself, and in this world of hyper-connectivity, we need to understand the importance of diversity, inclusion, and collaboration. Everyone is unique and has life experiences, skills and talents, and other resources that are accumulating in their personal wheelhouse ready to be accessed by others. In addition, most people are willing to give of their own resources if they are approached in a trusting manner. Since it is in our inherent nature to give of our trusted relationships with others, there is a treasure chest of potential connections that may have access to needed resources. These resources may be accessed and used to change the world and make a tremendous impact. So, hold dear your relationships, keep them intact, recognize their value, and proactively seek out new relationships with others. Who knows, at some point, you may be able to connect and bring those relationships to fruition in the form of an outside resource to something that is really important to you. In whatever form it may take, our trusted relationships are vital, and they serve as a conduit to other resources that may benefit the object of our passion and allow us to make an even more significant and intentional impact with our giving.

As you volunteer your time and leverage your talents to the maximum, it is essential to understand and keep high your "awareness antenna" for other needs and resources of the organization. The relationships that you have may serve as a conduit to other resources for this organization. It is crucial to understand that when you reach out to engage someone for an outside resource, that your approach is based on trust—seeking a win-win—for both parties. What is important in trusting relationships is understanding the motivations and needs of the other person through transparency and disclosure. If you clearly understand the cores of a trusted personal relationship based on integrity, intent, capabilities, and results, then you have someone that you can engage and enlist for an even greater impact!

By seeking a win-win, synergistic, mutually beneficial collaboration, you match your purpose or need with their mission and motivation. This is what we mean about trusting relationships. Please know it is not about you or them. It is about a mutually beneficial, synchronistic, reciprocal giving, teaming relationship for a *common* goal. Hence, to successfully engage and enlist trusting relationships and bring them to the table requires emotional intelligence to recognize the collaborative value in pursuit of the common cause.

In a nutshell...

- The answer to our *How?* varies depending on our personal situation and our giving wheelhouse of time, talents, trusted relationships, and treasure.
- Recognize that smart, practical, impactful giving is hard work and may be complex.
- If you are a good financial steward, money can serve as an excellent tool for benefitting your family, perpetuate personal values, create a personal and family legacy, and improve the causes that are important to you.

- Engaging and enlisting trusted relationships in a win-win manner can gain access to other resources and multiply the intended impact in pursuit of a common goal.

End of Chapter Exercise:

For each of my gifts listed below, possible answers to *How?* are:

My Time:_____

_____

My Talents:_____

_____

My Trusted Relationships:_____

_____

My Financial Resources:_____

_____

CHAPTER **13**

How Much to Give?

Balancing Financial & Emotional Security with Personal Meaning

Before you take your first swing in the giving stadium, let's take a moment to reflect on your gifts for giving. Having answered the essential questions of *Why?*, *Who?*, *What?*, *When?*, *Where?* and *How?*, let's look at how much to give (here after referred to *How much?*). As we tackle the *How much?*, we must break down the ways we can give of our time, talents, trust, and treasure.

Time: We give our time to develop trusting relationships, innovate with new ideas, create and implement impactful programs, and ultimately achieve lasting results. We invest our time in obtaining an education, developing new job skills, and in building trust in relationships. Spending our time in building relationships—whether they be relationships within our family or relationships with others—can help us become better versions of ourselves. We become better teachers, educators, mentors, coaches, spiritual and inspirational leaders, and lay the foundation by which we then make vibrant and prosperous families and communities.

So how much time should we invest in the passions and causes that are important to us? Time as an overall component of our giving plan is the same for us all. We all have 1440 minutes in a day—24 hours. How do you divide your time amongst all the demands of daily living? How do you split your time amongst your family, yourself, your job, and the giving to others? The answer is inevitably personal once again.

Our recognition that time is one of our most valuable assets leads to yet another personal assessment: what are my priorities? In summary, the giving of our time may ultimately boil down to the following personal assessment:

"Volunteers do not necessarily have the time; they just have the heart."

- Elizabeth Andrew

This quote sums up so eloquently the idea that while time is a precious resource, where there is a will, there is a way. If your heart is in it and it is a priority for you, you will make time.

Let's say you have made a personal assessment and that you can give three hours per week of your time. The answer will be different for everyone. Recognizing that time is one of our most valuable assets, we will each have to decide how to schedule our time in the best way possible. The end uses of our "free" time could be to family, including parents, spouse, children, and grandchildren. The giving of time could be to our job and career. The giving of time could be for self-development or for service that transcends self, work, and family. Be conscious, aware, and strategic in the giving of your time based on your priorities—guided by your giving heart and thinking head.

In summary, the personal gifting of our time is a highly personal and individual decision. But it is a precious gift. Therefore, we each should take some reflective time to determine how much we give of our time to others. The allocation of our time is a uniquely individual decision.

Talents and Trust: When it comes to talents and trusted relationships, the answer to *How much?* is pretty straightforward. When we go through the discovery process, we intentionally align our passions with our purpose. We then intentionally align our gifts in our giving wheelhouse with this united purpose and passion. We wholeheartedly bring our trusted connections that can help further the mission of the cause we are fully vested in. We realize that the gifting of our trusted relationships will bring additional resources to our cause. These trusted relationships bring their own set of wheelhouse gifts! We often overlook this gift in our wheelhouse. This specific gift of trusting relationships may unleash the dormant potential of others and open new horizons. We invite others to join a common cause for additional help, to access resources, and engage collaborators. We will then do good, facilitate positive momentum, and better our communities.

We understand through a personal assessment or with the help of a philanthropy coach that the talents, experiences, skill sets, and wisdom we bring to our passion are an essential form of giving. When we reach out and engage trusted relationships and align our talents with our emotions, we realize that deep personal meaning. We give it our all and the answer to *How much?* is simple. We bring 100% of our connected, trusting relationships and talents.

The crucial observation in this personal reflection is to recognize that we each have talents and trusted relationships to contribute. What is of the utmost importance here is ensuring your discovery process is thorough and accurate to align your skills and trusted relationships with your passions. Then giving it your all will naturally follow.

Treasure: In seeking the answer to *How much?* we have now covered three of the four personal gifts for giving. Financial wealth is the remaining gift in our wheelhouse. This question is posed as a "money" question but deals with the financial resources that we have available to us individually, which goes beyond cash. These financial resources take many forms to include investments, real estate, business assets, and other nontraditional financial resources. Some of these financial assets may be in the form of in-kind donations, gently used property, and collectibles. All of these are part of our financial resources—our treasure, "money."

Money, or treasure, as another word for our financial resources, is very close and personal to us. It is genuine and the most concrete of the gifts we all have to give. It is also vital to our daily lives. We need money as a means of exchange and for our current and future financial security, which does not always address our aspiration to give except in a minimal way depending on individual circumstances. Because money is so relevant to us in our daily living and is so real, it is probably top-of-mind when we ask ourselves, "How much can I give?"

The question of *How much?* raises yet another, more fundamental and straightforward question that addresses the role of money in our lives. This direct question is: "What is money for?" Is your money to be used as a tool and means to achieve a purpose-driven, financially secure life? Or, for those fortunate enough to have enough financial resources, is the goal simply the accumulation of more money? If we take a moment for personal reflection, we may realize that we may be accumulating more wealth than what we need for individual and family financial security. If you survey our current cultural landscape, media of all kinds often promotes and highlights the accumulation of excess wealth. Society portrays the amassing of wealth as a goal onto itself. In addition to the media focus on accumulation, professional wealth and financial advisors may encourage their clients to accumulate excess financial wealth in the form of investments and retirement savings. The professional wealth advisor encouragement is understandable since most professional financial and wealth advisors are compensated based on fees derived from their "assets under management."

Let me share with you a simple analogy that may help you better understand the role of money. Let's say you own a tree farm. Do you grow the trees just to grow them? Or, is the ultimate goal to harvest the timber from the trees for lumber that will be used to build? Amassing excess wealth is like growing a tree. We want to grow and use our money to create a purpose-driven, financially secure life. Money is the tool—the analogous tree—that enables us to "build" by giving, transforming, building, and serving a cause that is personally purposeful and meaningful.

As a preface to understanding the gifting of our money, let's clarify what we mean by our financial resources. Personal financial resources can take on several forms. The first thing that probably comes to mind is our monthly income, checking accounts, savings accounts, and investments that are accessible to us to spend or give or save. These "liquid," or readily easy-to-spend financial assets, are what we typically think of when we think of our money. Other kinds of assets that are part of our wealth include our homes, vacation homes (if we are so fortunate to have one), land, other real estate, and business assets. Other assets may consist of collectibles such as art or jewelry. From a financial planning perspective, these financial resources are all listed and valued on your balance sheet or your net worth statement.

It is important to note that some of these financial resources are what we call "liquid," or easy to turn into cash for the purchase of a product or service. Some of these financial resources, such as real estate, business property, and collectibles, are not liquid. If we are to use these more complex, non-liquid assets for gifting, then we need to take additional steps to convert them to a liquid form; a form that we can readily exchange for products and services. In this context, these non-liquid assets may be more suitable for planned giving strategy that can create both a living and a lasting legacy.

The question remains, "How much can I give financially?" In surveying the current philanthropic landscape there are few tools to help donors answer this layered and complex question. Vague answers to the financial *How much?* such as the giving of a percent of net worth are not particularly useful for charitable donors. Financial tithing based on personal income is one common method; especially amongst the faith traditions. For many, their financial priorities are their personal and family's financial security. Once these needs are met, additional thought may be given to charitable giving. What this means to each of us is dependent on our own personal and family financial situation. The decision to financially give becomes a balancing act between financial security and the emotional, good-heart-feeling satisfaction of giving.

Let's review the existing tools to answer the financial *How much?*. First, let's look at financial planning software as it addresses the question of how much to give. After spending 20 years as a financial planner helping individuals prepare for, transition into, and enjoy their retirement, I have found that many retirees manifest a great desire to financially give to their families and charity. Many advisors do not have what we call the "philanthropic conversation" with their clients. In fact, according to the most recent U.S. Trust Study of the Philanthropic Conversation, only 45% of high net worth (HNW) clients are satisfied with the charitable conversations with their advisors. A high-net-worth individual is usually defined as those with $1,000,000 or more in investable assets or with an income of greater than $250,000 per year. Assuming they and their families are financially secure, the HNW want to know how much they could comfortably give. Sadly, both the financial planning software currently available and professional advisors are laser-focused on retirement preparedness, retirement cash flow, and financial security and for the most part overlook financial giving. Current financial planning software addresses giving to family or charity only in a peripheral and superficial way. There is a glaring lack of professional advisor knowledge and software available that helps donors—those with a giving heart—calculate how much they can give financially. This is understandable since most wealth managers grow their revenues (and income) by growing their asset base, not by encouraging their clients to give assets away.

As a recap, there is little help to quantify how much to give. It always seems that people are asking for money. Various causes and nonprofits are asking for charitable donations to help meet their mission. Because those asking for money are typically from the nonprofit sector, they are not professionally qualified nor legally able to answer the question of *How much?*. Most professional advisors are also not in the position to quantify the answer to *How much?*. Hence, the answer to *How much?* is left up to the donor. Donors may not know what questions to ask of their professional advisors and are not willing to risk their personal and family financial security to pursue the answer to the *How much?*. For the donor, it is not worth the emotional risk to give more than they feel comfortable giving. What I have found is that the aspiration to give is alive and well, and more clients would like to engage in philanthropic conversations and ultimately quantify how much they could afford to give. In addition, most clients would prefer to give while living. After all, people like to have control and see the impact they would have with their giving and they can only see and feel the results of the beneficial impact while they are living.

In a nutshell...

- Be a good steward of your time and periodically review how you spend or invest your time.
- Recognize the value of your talents and relationships and give 100%.
- Set up a "spending budget" for your gifts of time and money.

End of Chapter Exercise:

For each of my gifts listed below, my *How much?* answer is:

My Time:_____

_____

My Talents:_____

_____

My Trusted Relationships:_____

_____

My Financial Resources:_____

_____

CHAPTER 14

A Summary of Key Take-Aways for Your Giving Journey

Resources for Your Personal Giving

We have covered a lot of territory in this book! We have introduced new concepts such as the life journey of aspirational giving, the Appreciative Donor Education Process, the giving heart and thinking head, the giving wheelhouse, and the seven essential questions for smart giving. Hopefully, you have been able to reflect on where you are on your life journey as well as find the answers to the seven questions for the gifting of your time, talents, treasure, and trust. Even though you may have laid the groundwork for your roadmap to successful giving, you may have more questions. Don't panic! Your giving heart has been awakened, you have new interest and motivation to realize your giving dreams, and you now have the framing questions and format to design and deliver to benefit your family and those causes that are really important to you.

In this chapter, we will wrap it all up in the hopes of making it clearer, simpler, and easier to understand. Our hope at Aspire to Give is to help you unleash your giving spirit and potential for social good and to achieve more meaning in life. This is not an easy process and it takes time to do it right. Traditionally, the giving heart—you, the donor—has had to figure out giving on your own. If you as a donor were to seek out guidance for giving to family or charity, you may turn to professional advisors for guidance. While they may be experts in their particular field (accounting, finance, law), most professional advisors have limited expertise in philanthropic giving. Their primary focus is on their area of specialty such as investments, tax strategies, or the preparation of legal documents. What I have found in developing the Appreciative Donor Education Process is that—first and foremost—it is the giving from the heart. It is the emotional answer to the *Why?* that clarifies the reason the donor would like to give to a specific cause or passion that is important to him or her. Most professional advisors do not engage is finding the answer to your *Why?*. This leads to another concept that reinforces the need for both inside ("family") and outside (professional) guidance and counsel.

First, let's talk about you—the giving heart that really wants to make a difference. You are the key to unlocking your own potential and making that difference. It is up to you to steer your own ship with your gifts for giving. While you may seek additional guidance from a sounding board, spouse, confidant, philanthropy coach, or from professional advisors, it is really up to you to navigate your own philanthropic giving journey and steer your giving ship to achieve the dreams of impact, benefit, and transformation that you envision. You steer the gifts from your giving wheelhouse. I strongly suggest that you find a competent and trusted first mate that will serve as a navigator to help chart your course.

The Role of
Trusted Professional Advisors

As previously noted, you along with your first mate are the captain of your giving ship as you seek to give from your wheelhouse. There are numerous philanthropic conversations worth having to engage both your giving heart and your thinking head. Besides your first mate, you may want to seek outside guidance as part of these conversations. Typically, we think of professional advisors as accountants, attorneys, insurance professionals, or investment professionals. You also may engage in conversations with nonprofit executive directors, development professionals, counselors, and faith-based clergy.

So, as a good steward and captain of your giving ship, it is also important to ask questions of your advisors and counselors. These questions should be focused on receiving their guidance; as well as understanding their perspective, intent, competency, limitations, and concern to do what is in your best interest.

No matter what kind of professional guidance you seek, it is important to understand that the effectiveness and importance of the philanthropic conversation may be affected by one of these three factors:

- Expertise
- Comfort with the philanthropic conversation
- Intent

Expertise

In looking at professional advisors and counselors, many are experts in their specific field. These professionals typically include estate attorneys, accountants, bankers, financial planners, insurance, investment, and other professionals. They are typically highly skilled in their profession but may not have the specific expertise in philanthropic giving. As a professional, they may not want to admit their lack of expertise, or frankly, do not know what they do not know. Hopefully, your professional advisor recognizes their limitations and can refer you to a philanthropy coach or some other trusted professional.

As an example, a high income or high net worth donor approaches their personal attorney and wants to "give back" to the local community. The estate attorney may have experience in setting up a private foundation and can provide the legal guidance and documents. However, the attorney may not have a meaningful discussion of ALL the various options (other than a private foundation) available to a donor. The estate attorney knows that fees will be charged to set up and provide on-going legal guidance for the foundation and may not discuss possible alternatives such as a Donor Advised Fund (DAF) or the variations of charitable trusts.

Comfort with the Philanthropic Conversation

As expected, discussing philanthropic giving from your wheelhouse is a highly personal conversation. As you may recall from chapter 6 there is wide variety of the types of conversations using the seven essential questions. Some philanthropic conversations include conversations of the heart (*Why?*) and other conversations are more practical (*When?, What?, How?, How much?*). While most professional advisors are comfortable talking within their comfort zone of their expertise (law, taxes, investments, etc.), having the softer, interpersonal skills and emotional intelligence to approach and engage in a philanthropic conversation of the heart is totally different. Many professional advisors may not be comfortable with, know how, or think it is their role to engage in a philanthropic conversation with you. Professional advisors typically do not take the time to understand what is really important to you and what you care about. Most professional advisors are not professionally trained in approaching and engaging in this type of conversation.

As an example, a donor is discussing their tax situation with their accountant. Of course, the accountant's expertise is "numbers and taxes," and while the accountant may be comfortable discussing tax saving charitable strategies, a more in-depth conversation on the donor's charitable giving may be out of the normal "comfort zone" of the accountant.

Intent

Lastly, in working with professional advisors, it is always important to understand the professional's intent since there may be a potential conflict of interest, even amongst fee-only professional advisors. For example, if a wealth manager is paid based on fees generated from assets-under-management (AUM), the wealth manager may be reluctant to discuss the giving of money; whether that be giving to family or charity. If the client were to give to a charity from the assets being managed, it would reduce the compensation of the advisor: i.e. fewer assets (AUM) means less revenues.

So, how do you assess philanthropic giving-guidance professionals?

As a first step and with the help of your first mate or philanthropy coach, review the discovery and dream steps of the philanthropic giving process and confirm your answers to the *Why?*, *Who?* and *Where?*.

As a second step, you should assess whether your professional advisors (accountant, attorney, financial/wealth advisor, etc.) have philanthropic giving expertise. Can they expertly address all the questions you have on your giving? Do they understand you as a person and what motivates you to give? Are there any potential conflicts of interest? Are both you and your advisors comfortable having the conversations? Has your advisor initiated the philanthropic conversation with you? If not, *Why?*

As an additional step, you may want to search out and find a subscription-based, fee-only philanthropy coach or philanthropic advisor that will serve as a fiduciary to serve in your best interest. In most cases a fee only Certified Financial Planner® (CFP®) that is also a Chartered Advisor in Philanthropy® (CAP®) may be the best credentialed combination that will serve as a fiduciary and always act in your best interest. Your philanthropy coach or advisor should also be willing to serve as your philanthropic quarterback and collaborate with your other advisors as needed.

It is also important to ask questions of advisors that are compensated by fees generated by assets under management. It is important to understand the inherent conflict of interest in such an arrangement. Please be sure to meet with, ask questions, seek full transparency, and ask for the full disclosure of fees and any conflicts of interest. Will they serve as a fiduciary that will always act in your best interest?

To sum it up, you have a giving heart and you listen and engage your thinking head as you work through the five-step appreciative donor education process. It is vitally important to find a trusted first mate to accompany you on your giving journey that can serve as a sounding board for you. Find and turn to additional trustworthy crew as needed such as nonprofit professionals, counselors, and professional advisors. Do not be afraid to ask questions and take your time when you are making giving decisions. Lastly, realize that with self-reflection and help from others you can achieve smart, impactful, heart-felt giving that will bring you great meaning and joy in life that will provide both a living and lasting legacy.

What are you waiting for? Let's go do some good!

About the Author

Greg Doepke is the founder of Aspire to Give®, a social enterprise dedicated to unleashing the human spirit to advance philanthropy through donor education, social innovation, collaboration, and advocacy. Greg serves as the Philanthropist in Residence at Auburn University's Cary Center for the Advancement of Philanthropy and Nonprofit  studies. He serves on the Board of Directors for the International Association for Advisors in Philanthropy as well. As a West Point graduate with a passion for servant leadership and credentialed expertise in all facets of financial, estate and philanthropic planning, Greg is committed to raising the philanthropic literacy for others as a means to better ourselves, our families, our local communities and our nation.

Greg is married to Suzette, a shining example of a giving heart who is the inspiration for Aspire, the avatar of the Giving Heart for Aspire to Give®. Suzette is a retired kindergarten teacher who continues to exemplify what it means to be a giving heart, not just with her family and friends, but others within the community. Suzette and Greg have two caring daughters, seven thriving grandchildren, and the couple happily resides in Auburn, Ala.